MW00475668

Revolutionary
WESTMINSTER

Revolutionary
WESTMINSTER

from Massacre to Statehood

JESSIE HAAS

Charleston   London

THE
History
PRESS

Published by The History Press
Charleston, SC 29403
www.historypress.net

Copyright © 2011 by the Westminster Historical Society
All rights reserved

Front Cover: The Cumberland County Courthouse from *Vermont, the Green Mountain State*,
by Walter Hill Crockett.
Back Cover, left: Tory Tavern, *courtesy of the Westminster Historical Society;*
right: Margaret Schoolcraft, *courtesy of Fort Ticonderoga Museum.*

First published 2011

Manufactured in the United States

ISBN 978.1.60949.166.6

Library of Congress Cataloging-in-Publication Data
Haas, Jessie.
Revolutionary Westminster : from massacre to statehood / Jessie Haas.
p. cm.
Includes bibliographical references and index.
ISBN 978-1-60949-166-6
1. Westminster (Vt.)--History--18th century. 2. Westminster (Vt.)--History, Military--18th
century. 3. Westminster (Vt.)--Politics and government--18th century. 4. Massacres--
Vermont--Westminster--History--18th century. 5. Vermont--History--Revolution, 1775-
1783. I. Title.
F59.W5H33 2011
974.3'9--dc22
2010050610

Notice: The information in this book is true and complete to the best of our knowledge. It is
offered without guarantee on the part of the author or The History Press. The author and
The History Press disclaim all liability in connection with the use of this book.

All rights reserved. No part of this book may be reproduced or transmitted in any form
whatsoever without prior written permission from the publisher except in the case of brief
quotations embodied in critical articles and reviews.

"Red Westminster"
A Small Town in the American Revolution

But Vengeance let us Wreak, my Boys,
For Matron, Maid, and Spinster:
Whose joys are fled, whose Homes are sad,
For the Youth of Red Westminster.[1]
—from an anonymous ballad published in 1779

Contents

Date _10 510 6-111_

M _____

Address _____

Reg. No.	Clerk	Account Forward		
1				
2				
3	9781609491666		19 99	
4				
5	9780312681944		25 99	
6				
7				
8			45 98	
9				
10	tax		2 76	
11				
12				
13				
14	06833-31			
15			48 74	

35   Your Account Stated to Date - If Error is Found, Return at Once

THANK YOU
Call Again

We appreciate your patronage and
hope we may continue to merit it.
If we please you, tell your friends.
If we don't, tell us.
We strive to satisfy.

Acknowledgements

This project was made possible through generous funding from the Dascomb Trust. George B. Dascomb, founder of the trust, was a descendant of many of the founders of Westminster.

The Westminster Historical Society commissioned a new history of Westminster; this book is an outgrowth of that work. The Board of Directors has been most supportive throughout, and I thank them for giving me this fascinating opportunity. Board member Dan Axtell offered valuable technical help. My father, Bob Haas, also on the Historical Society Board, loaned many materials from his library. Karen Larson and Michael Fawcett took photos. Christopher D. Fox at Fort Ticonderoga and Jackie Calder and Paul Carnahan at the Vermont Historical Society enabled the use of images from their collections.

Finally, utmost thanks to the indispensable Alice Caggiano. Without her organizational skills and knowledge of the Westminster Historical Society collection, this work would have taken four or five times longer to complete. Alice, you rock!

The Westminster Historical Society Board honors Marie Wright, Frank Walter and Hank Anderson, who passed away within the last year as this book was being conceived and written. All contributed greatly to the historical society and to Westminster.

Introduction
Guns at Midnight

March 13, 1775. Atop a wooded bluff, candlelight gleams in the windows of the Cumberland County Courthouse, and young men armed with wooden staves joke and jostle, trying to stay awake. A few hours ago, one hundred of them faced a sheriff's posse outside these doors, armed with flintlock rifles, and it looked like there would be a fight. But militia captain Azariah Wright negotiated with smooth-talking Judge Thomas Chandler to allow them to occupy the courthouse overnight unmolested. Most of their companions have dispersed to find supper and beds, leaving about thirty men on guard.

It's a big drama for a small frontier town. Westminster village, which occupies a terrace above the Connecticut River, consists of a straight road a mile long and ten rods wide, called the King's Highway, with a dozen or so homesteads ranged on either side of it. At the northern end of the street, the meetinghouse stands in the center of the King's Highway; a few hundred yards north of it, at the edge of the bluff, sits the Cumberland County Courthouse, the center of New York colonial government at the border with New Hampshire. Below, the King's Highway runs straight as a gun barrel for another mile between homesteads, fields and woods. To the west are more homesteads scattered in the hills. Westminster's been settled for about fifteen years. It's a raw little place, but it is the county seat. That's brought importance, and in these uneasy times when war seems to be brewing with Great Britain, it's brought trouble, too.

Lights twinkle dimly on the plain below, half a mile north. That's the Tory Tavern, where Sheriff Paterson has taken his posse. The men on guard feel a little wistful about that. The sheriff's men are down there lapping up rum, while up here we're freezing our—

What's that? You hear something? A stick breaks. Feet trample up the steep slope of Courthouse Hill. A musket barrel gleams in the moonlight.

"Man the doors! Man the doors!"

The defenders crowd the walk before the courthouse door as a body of men rushes forward, bristling with guns. They're only ten rods away when Sheriff Paterson shouts, "Take aim! Fire!"

Three scattered shots; musket balls thunk into the lintel above the door. Before the unarmed crowd on the walkway can react, Paterson roars, "Fire, Goddamn ye! Fire! Send them to hell!"

The night blazes red with gunfire. There are men down, men falling over them, yelling, groaning, swearing. Some defenders break for the side doors as the sheriff's men charge in, trampling the wounded on the floor.

Over the din Phil Safford shouts, "Don't run, boys! Don't run! We'll go out the same way as we came in!" Swinging his wooden staff like a cutlass, he fights his way through the sheriff's men, clubbing several down, taking saber cuts on the head from Paterson's sword.

Then he and a few others are out in the dark. They race down the hill to Captain Wright's house, half a mile away, passing the Tory Tavern where this treachery was hatched; they stagger in and tell their bloody tale. Wright, the soldier, the hothead, the man of strong opinions, who slaps the minister's face whenever they meet simply to express his dislike, doesn't hesitate for a moment. He sends for help: to Walpole, New Hampshire, to his hometown of Northfield in the Massachusetts Bay Colony. Reuben Jones rides hatless to Dummerston to rouse the militia there.

Meanwhile, the sheriff's posse pack their twenty-plus prisoners into a cell. One, William French, is shot in the head and mouth and is clearly dying. They drag him in by an arm and a leg. The cell is so tightly packed that his friends can't move to help him. His captors laugh at his moans and convulsions and refresh themselves at the courthouse bar.

They are triumphant, for tonight. Tomorrow, four hundred armed militiamen will be in the streets of this tiny frontier town, and civil government will be overthrown.

The Westminster Massacre is over. The revolution is just beginning.

Chapter 1
What Colony Is This?

R eally, it's a wonder that there was only one Westminster Massacre. Vermont towns were granted by three different colonies; Westminster alone had four charters. The new towns rapidly filled with war-toughened veterans, drawn from colonies already in a state of tension with Great Britain. A new king trying to close a budget deficit, growing sentiment for independence, jurisdictional confusion: Vermont was a revolutionary incident waiting to happen.

In the 1730s, New England colonies faced pressure to expand. Population growth was relentless. Farmland in southern New England was crowded and soils were depleted. Cash-strapped colonial governments owed compensation to vast numbers of former soldiers. Granting lands in northern New England was the obvious solution, as soon as the Indian threat diminished.

In 1735, during a period of relative calm, the Massachusetts General Assembly ordered a survey of land from Rumford to the Great Falls (present Bellows Falls). Present New Hampshire and Vermont were then considered part of Massachusetts Bay Colony. Twenty-eight six-mile-square townships were laid out between the Connecticut and Merrimack Rivers, and on November 19, 1736, Township Number One was granted to "a number of persons from Taunton, Norton, and Easton in Massachusetts, and from Ashford and Killingly in Connecticut."[2] (Rockingham; Charlestown, New Hampshire; and Chesterfield, New Hampshire, were granted at the same time.)

There's no evidence that Number One was ever a native settlement, but it may have been a graveyard. In 1896, a human skeleton was uncovered by a plow-man on a farm just south of the village, site of the first English homestead in Westminster. "The position of the body would indicate that [it] had been thrown into a hole and doubled together so as to occupy as little space as possible. No clue could be found which would lead to its identification." The body appeared to have been buried in too small a grave. "It was doubled up so that the head rested on or near the knees. The selectmen and doctors were summoned and a careful examination of the surroundings made. All agreed that the body has been buried for many years. The bones were buried again by the authorities so that they can be produced if wanted."

There was some talk that an "idiot" had lived on the farm, mistreated by a family and perhaps murdered. However, "George Foster, an old and respected resident of the town, says that 50 years ago…on nearly the same ground where this one was found he plowed up two skulls…These facts…go to show that this locality was undoubtedly the burial place of the Indians."[3] Many Native American remains of the Early and Middle Woodland period (900 BC to AD 1000) were buried in a flexed position, like the skeleton found at Westminster.[4] Two stone tools are documented as having been found in Westminster: an axe found near the old brickyard south of the east village and a pestle found at Grout station. Arrowheads dating to the Archaic period show that the land had been hunted for thousands of years.

Stone pestle (top) and axe found in Westminster. *Westminster Historical Society.*

But Number One was empty when the Massachusetts surveyors drew up lots. The land was promising: broad meadows on four terraces near the river, and to the west a wooded upland seamed north to south by three rocky ridges. Lots were assigned, and in 1739 the first settlers—Richard Ellis and his son Reuben, of Easton, Massachusetts—came to Number One, now called New Taunton. They broke up several acres of land and built a small house just south of the present village, an area with broad, fertile meadows, a small brook and useful clay deposits. One other house was built nearby.

No sooner were the houses built than, in March 1740, New Hampshire gained independence from Massachusetts. A long-standing dispute over the northern border of Massachusetts was settled; it now appeared that Township Number One was part of New Hampshire. Confused and discouraged, the proprietors of New Taunton gave up their project for over ten years.

Captain Josiah Willard, commander of Fort Dummer (present Brattleboro, Vermont) during Greylock's War (1723–27), had acquired twelve shares in the defunct New Taunton. Willard died in 1750. His son, Josiah Willard Jr., commander of the garrison at Ashuelot (now Keene, New Hampshire), inherited his command at Dummer and his shares in New Taunton. The Treaty of Aix-la-Chapelle ended the war between the French and English, Indian activity diminished and, in 1751, a few settlers ventured to New Taunton.

William Goold; his son John; his daughter Polly Carpenter and her husband Amos and children; and a friend, Atherton Chaffee, moved into the house built by Richard Ellis. The Goolds were from Northfield, Massachusetts. John, nineteen, was a blacksmith. Amos Carpenter, thirty-six, was a native of Rehoboth, Massachusetts, a millwright and a blacksmith. Atherton Chaffee, older than the others, had a wife and several children in Ashford, Connecticut. He also had substantial landholdings there. The Goold group was joined by John Averill, his pregnant wife, Mary, and their six children ranging from teenage to toddlers, who moved into the other house. Averill was a master carpenter, forty years old when he and his family paddled canoes upriver to New Taunton.

Goold brought the rest of his family up that summer. Old accounts of Westminster's settlement mention only heads of households, giving the impression of a male-dominated frontier enclave. But that first summer New Taunton was more like a family campground, with eight adults and at least a dozen children. In the fall, Mrs. Averill gave birth to a daughter, Anna, the first recorded birth in Westminster.

NEW CHARTER

New Hampshire's charter described the colony's borders as extending west "until it meet those of other governments." That was open to interpretation, and Benning Wentworth, New Hampshire's ambitious governor, interpreted freely. In his mind, the border extended to the Hudson Valley. New Yorkers believed their colony extended to the west bank of the Connecticut, and when Wentworth began granting towns in present Vermont, they protested to the Crown.

Meanwhile, on November 9, 1752, Wentworth re-granted Number One and changed its name to Westminster. In doing so, he re-created a bit of the landscape near London. At that time the English Westminster was an independent town; other towns in the vicinity were Putney and Fulham (the original name of Dummerston).[5] Major Josiah Willard Jr. was given the right to convene town meetings. Of the thirty-three proprietors under the second charter, only John Averill had ever lived in the new town. The proprietors voted to honor the old Massachusetts claims.

In 1753, war erupted again with the French. On August 30, 1754, Indians captured eight people in Charlestown, New Hampshire, a few miles north. Alarmed, the Westminster families crossed the river to Walpole and sheltered in the fortified house of Colonel Benjamin Bellows. They returned in October, but in February 1755, Chaffee and the Averills moved to Putney. With families from Putney and Westmoreland, they rebuilt an old fort on the Great Meadows, just over the border in Putney, previously occupied by woodcutters and scouts. The Averill children grew up in this military encampment, and the youngest was born there. The other Westminster families probably went back to Northfield. Westminster was abandoned for the second time.

It may have been at this time that Atherton Chaffee was set upon by Indians in the hills west of the village. Said to be a tall and powerful man, Chaffee ran to the river and pushed off in a canoe to midstream. The story was found among Bertha Miller Collins's papers.

These were violent years in the Connecticut Valley. In 1755, nineteen people living near Fort Dummer were killed or "captivated" by Indians. Massachusetts offered a bounty on Indian captives and scalps, and ranging parties known as "scalping designs" roamed southern Vermont.

Command of Fort Dummer was taken over by Nathan Willard, who installed three Westminster proprietors, Oliver, Wilder and William Willard, (four counting five-year-old Billy Willard, there with his parents), in the only large houses in the fort. Comfort for the Willards came at the expense of five other soldiers whose families were allegedly made to share two small rooms. They complained to the Massachusetts General Court; it's not known what action was taken.[6]

Indian attacks continued. In 1758, Colonel Ebenezer Hinsdell sent a letter to Governor Wentworth that closed with these words: "We are loath to tarry here merely to be killed."

In this dangerous year, 1758, Eleazer Harlow of Taunton, age twenty, settled in Westminster on the brow of what would become Courthouse Hill. (Harlows have lived in Westminster ever since.) Azariah Dickinson, of Haddam, Connecticut, and his pregnant wife, Temperance, also came. Their first son, Abraham, was born in Westminster in September 1758. Though Harlow and Dickinson were in Westminster concurrently, they weren't close neighbors. Dickinson and his brothers, Dan and Job, farmed in the southeast section of town, a couple of miles south of Courthouse Hill.

In 1759, the Indian threat greatly diminished. In Westminster, brothers Charles and Francis Holden, fifteen and sixteen years old, settled in the far southwest part of the township about six miles from Harlow. The brothers built bark lean-tos to live in while they cleared the land. They returned to Massachusetts for the winter, and when they came back in the spring of 1760, they brought their brides. According to Holden family lore, the teenaged couples were driven out of the first place they settled by "adder snakes." Descendants of the snakes and the Holdens still live on Windmill Hill.

The year 1760 saw the fall of Montreal and the final defeat of France. With the war over, the rich, unclaimed land of present-day Vermont drew speculators and homesteaders like ants to a picnic. Benning Wentworth resumed making grants in January 1760. Josiah Willard Jr. obtained a renewal of Westminster's charter from Wentworth on June 11, 1760. The Averills, Chaffee and other 1754 families moved back.

In 1760 they were joined by a friend from the Great Meadows fort. Captain Michael Gilson was thirty years old and had been a soldier half his life. Now the veteran was ready to settle down. About a mile north of Fort Hill, he put up a log cabin on the scenic height overlooking the Connecticut Valley. Soon after that he married Sarah Sessions, a sister of John Sessions. The Sessions family were neighbors, just settling in southeast Westminster.

William Willard also moved to Westminster in 1760. William was a cousin and brother-in-law of Josiah Willard Jr., having married Josiah's sister Prudence. William and Prudence's ten-year-old son, Billy, was also a Westminster proprietor, as were Prudence's brothers Oliver, Nathan and

Wilder and her brother-in-law, John Arms. William's father had been killed in an Indian attack the very day he was to have assumed the pastorate of Rutland, Massachusetts, when William was three. William became a soldier garrisoned at Fort Dummer and Fort Hill in Putney. His wife joined him at his posts with their children; Billy was born at Fort Dummer about 1750. The Willards lived on the land settled by Richard Ellis in 1739. Gilson, Sessions and Willard would play prominent roles in the drama to come.

Other settlers rapidly joined them. Many had checked out the river meadows during the war and liked what they saw. A handwritten account by Hollis Wright, son of Medad Wright, tells the story of a few settlers who would become important to Westminster's story.

> *Account of the settlement of the "upper street"*
> *My father, Mr. Holton, Mr. McNaughton Norton (that was the way he spelled his name, now spelled Norton) and two others were soldiers in the French war stationed at Hossock and were…orted to take provisions over to No 4. they crossed from Hossock to Northfield Mass and took canoes up the river one night they camped on the meddows (which were covered with heavy [...er?]…they were pleased with the spot and agreed after the war to settle there. accordingly after the war was over they met at Northfield and went up the river in a canoe (without their families) and landed in the mouth of the creek below the present village of W, and walked up to the spot…where the house of D.C. now stands and made their camp and made their clame. McNoughton where he afterwards built his famous tavern (now standing owned by Mr. Brigham) Wright on the spot where the camp stood and where he build a log house near where and…where his son and granddson lived. Holton on the spot now owned by his grand daughter Mrs. S.S. Stodard. one of the others spitched [?] his claim about a mile above the others about a mile below on what is now known as the lower street. they worked their claims and at night came to the camp they afterwards brought their families and others settled there among them Azariah Wright (brother of the first Wright) who settled between his brother and Holton.[7]*

Among the men who came from Northfield in 1761 were Medad and Azariah Wright, their cousin Benjamin Burt, John Norton and Joel Holton. Burt took up land in north Westminster. The others settled near one another. The Holton lot was on the north corner of Sand Hill Road, and the Azariah Wright lot was on the south corner. Medad was next south, and John Norton built his home on a slight rise south of Medad.

Benjamin Burt of Northfield, twenty years old, was a veteran of the Ticonderoga, Crown Point and Montreal expeditions. He settled in the far northern part of Westminster and built a house and sawmill near the mouth of Saxton's River.

Joel Holton, twenty-two years old, married Bethia Farwell and raised twelve children with her while farming and starting Westminster's first sawmill.

John Norton was of Scotch-Irish descent, the family name in Ireland being McNaughten. When he moved to Westminster, he changed his name to Norton and after that was deeply offended to be called by his old name. Once he had cleared his farmstead, Norton built a large house, which he established as a tavern.

Medad Wright, twenty-seven, a shoemaker, and his brother Azariah, twenty-four, a mason, were third cousins to both Benjamin Burt and Ethan Allen. (In 1653, at age twenty-four, Samuel Wright married Elizabeth Burt, with whom he had eight children. In 1667, his brother Judah married Elizabeth's sister Mercy, a child of five on her older sister's wedding day. Judah and Mercy's great-grandsons were Ira and Ethan Allen. Samuel's great-grandsons were Medad and Azariah Wright of Westminster. Benjamin Burt descended from a brother of Elizabeth and Mercy Burt.)

All were veterans and hardworking farmers, but Azariah was something more. Historian Benjamin Hall said, "Noted for the boldness of his nature, and the eccentricity of his conduct," he was "peculiarly fitted for the rough life of a pioneer." Wright's own great-grandson, Henry C. Lane, said, "Combined with Capt. Wright's patriotism was a vein of eccentricity that amounted almost to insanity."[8]

Medad Wright and John Norton married sisters of Joel Holton. Azariah Wright married Mary Safford, a sister of Lieutenant Philip Safford of Rockingham. These young ex-soldiers built small houses, cleared their farms and began to raise families. This one family enclave represented the range of political opinion in Westminster. While Holton kept his nose out of politics, the Tory John Norton, the Yorkers Medad Wright and Benjamin Burt and the activist Whig Azariah Wright would all be actors in Westminster's primary drama.

Other important settlers included Ephraim Ranney, who came to Westminster from Middletown, Connecticut, in 1761 with his wife, Silence, their children and his brother-in-law Ephraim. Ranney built a tavern near the river; Ephraim Wilcox settled in the West Parish.

The Burk family—Jonathan Burk, his three sons, Jesse, Simeon and Silas, and their households—came from Brimfield, Massachusetts. Jesse was married to a widow named Rice, whose first husband had been killed by Indians. She had a three-year-old son, Charles Rice, when the family came to Westminster.

CADWALLADER COLDEN

In 1761, the same year the Wrights came to Westminster, Cadwallader Colden was appointed lieutenant governor of New York. Colden, a Scottish-born physician, mathematician, botanist, physicist, author and inventor, held his new post for the rest of his life and was frequently acting governor when governors died, appointments lapsed or gubernatorial trips to Britain were necessary. Colden was a royalist who deeply distrusted New Englanders. He didn't like their republicanism, their forms of self-government or their grasping large sections of his fiefdom. Under his rule, the border problem with New Hampshire became a live issue.

Benning Wentworth granted thirty-six new townships west of the Connecticut in 1763, selling Colden's colony out from under him. In a September 1763 letter to the British lords of trade contesting the westward extension of the Massachusetts boundary, Colden wrote:

> The New England Governments are formed in republican principles and these principles are zealously inculcated on their youth, in opposition to the principles of the Constitution of Great Britain. The government of New York, on the contrary, is established as nearly as may be, after the model of the English Constitution. Can it then be good policy to diminish the extent of jurisdiction in His Majesty's province of New York, to extend the power and influence of the others?[9]

On December 23, 1763, Colden proclaimed in a letter to his own officials that New York writ ran to the banks of the Connecticut "notwithstanding any contrarity of jurisdiction claimed by the government of New Hampshire." He ordered the sheriff of Albany County (at that time including all of present Vermont) to provide the New York government with the names of all settlers squatting on New York land under a New Hampshire grant. This would have included every person in Westminster.

Wentworth issued a counter-proclamation, scoffing at New York's claim and predicting that His Majesty would confirm his grants. He ordered his own officials to consider the Grants theirs to police and granted, by autumn of 1764, five more towns.

But the Privy Council had finally gotten around to settling the dispute. On July 26, 1764, His Majesty declared "the western banks of the river Connecticut...to be the boundary line between the two said provinces of New Hampshire and New York."

"To be." What did those words mean?

If they meant "is and always has been," then the settlers who'd bought their lands under grants from New Hampshire were squatters, without rights. If they meant "from now on," then settlers with New Hampshire grants should be grandfathered into New York State, with rights and protections under British law.

In the 1760s, the Crown likely meant the latter. Many warnings were handed to the New York government that seem clearly intended to protect the poor and hardworking settlers of the Grants. Official New York documents honored those warnings with a striking appearance of humanity and fairness. The reality was different and varied depending on who was governor. Colden wrote brilliantly humane public documents while granting large tracts west of the Green Mountains to his friends and cronies. There was frequent friction between New Hampshire grantees and New York officials, as well as escalating violence.

East of the mountains, life was quieter. Brattleboro and Guilford were strongly sympathetic to New York's claim; Rockingham, Dummerston and Putney tended to favor New Hampshire; and in Westminster, opinion was mixed. The town had already seen jurisdiction pass from Massachusetts to New Hampshire and had experienced how these difficulties could be smoothed out among powerful and prosperous men. New York was far away, and so was New York law. The cultural abrasions weren't pressing if you didn't run across Yorkers every day.

Anyway, the whole thing might not be settled yet. Governor John Wentworth, succeeding his uncle Benning in 1766, wasn't resigned to losing half his territory. Westminster citizens took a wait-and-see approach, sometimes signing petitions seeking New Hampshire citizenship and other times turning to New York. "Just settle it so I don't lose my farm" would seem to have been the prevailing attitude.

Meanwhile, a new king was on the throne. George III inherited a country deep in debt. The French and Indian War had cost Britain a fortune. Some of that money was spent defending the American colonists; George and his ministers considered it only fair that the colonies pick up a share of the financial burden. But the colonies had been ruled with a light hand up till now and had not been taxed. King George's attempts to raise revenues—starting with older measures like the Navigation Acts, long on the books but never enforced—came as a shock.

In 1765, the king went further. The Grenville Acts clamped down on the colonial wool trade to protect the domestic British wool industry; reserved colonial raw materials, especially timber, for the navy and merchant marine; restricted trade in hats and iron between the colonies; raised duties on sugar, molasses and other products from outside Britain; and gave royal officials jurisdiction over taxation and customs.

The colonists were incredulous. They had borne the physical hardships of this war themselves. They weren't used to being taxed, they lacked representation in Parliament and given the distances and difficulty of communication, they'd begun to think that true representation was impossible.

The Stamp Act, one element of the Grenville Acts, particularly inflamed public opinion. Threats and mob violence forced every stamp agent in the thirteen colonies to resign within a year of the law's enactment. None of this touched Westminster directly, but it created a rebellious atmosphere in the colonies that spread to the Grants with new settlers.

Cumberland County

In the 1760s, Vermont was part of Albany County. At such distances, over bad roads, New York law was effectively nonexistent. That was felt to be a burden by some Vermont settlers, and in 1766, their petitions to the New York legislature produced Cumberland County, New York, encompassing present Windham, Windsor and parts of Orange Counties.

Local courts were established, civil and military officers were appointed (not elected) and roads and taxes were established. The new county had a rudimentary courthouse and jail, located in Chester through the earnest petitions of Judge Thomas Chandler, who lived there. A court of common pleas was held annually. Courts of general sessions were held twice yearly, in June and November.

Re-re-re-Grant

In 1766, New York's council ordered all New Hampshire grant holders to acquire confirmatory New York patents within three months.[10] New fees were demanded, which came as a shock in a cash-poor economy.

New Hampshire town grants came cheap—roughly 20 pounds sterling, with towns averaging approximately fifteen thousand acres. The annual quitrent to the king was a shilling per one hundred acres. The New York fee was 14 pounds sterling per thousand acres, which worked out to about 330 pounds sterling for the average township, more than fifteen times the New Hampshire price. Quitrent was two shillings sixpence per hundred acres, more than twice as much.

A group of Grants landholders clubbed together and sent one of their own to London to plead for them. Their petition describes their "utter astonishment" at the New York fees, "which being utterly unable to do and perform, We find ourselves reduced to the sad Necessity of losing all our past Expense and Advancements, and many of us being reduced to absolute Poverty and Want, having expended Our All in making said Settlements."

The more moderate terms of the New Hampshire grants were seen by the petitioners as an inducement to settle even on "the more rough and unprofitable parts of said Lands." They feared that the high cost of New York grants would prevent "the full and proper Settlement of said Country, and on the Whole to the lessening of your Majesty's Revenue." The consequences painted by these petitioners were dire: "And so the (Lands) will fall into the Hands of the Rich, to be taken up, the more valuable parts only as aforesaid, and these perhaps not entered upon and settled for many years to come; while your petitioners with their numerous and helpless Families, will be obliged to wander far and wide to find where to plant themselves down, so as to be able to live."[11]

The Society for the Propagation of the Gospel (SPG) also took an interest, liking the free lots for church glebe and the SPG itself in the New Hampshire charters. At the SPG's instigation, the Privy Council ordered New York not to issue any more grants "until his Majesty's further Pleasure shall be known."

New York complied for two years; meanwhile, New Hampshire titleholders launched a major initiative to sell cheap New Hampshire titles. The more families on the land, the harder it would be to overturn the grants. The population swelled. In 1766, there were 50 families in Westminster. By 1771, when New York ordered a census, Westminster was the most populous town in this part of the province with 478 residents. Guilford and Brattleboro were next in size, followed by Putney and Rockingham.

Jay Mack Holbrook[12] notes, "Usually high-growth, frontier populations are associated with youthfulness and an excess of males." Westminster had 136 boys under age fifteen, 107 men ages sixteen to fifty-nine, 8 men over age sixty, 107 girls under age fifteen and 117 women ages sixteen and over. There were no blacks.

There were twenty-nine more boys than girls in Westminster. A girl could be pretty sure of getting married in this town; a boy might have to court elsewhere. Boys also outnumbered men by the same margin. Old men were very few. Women outnumbered girls, though the number of women fifty-nine and older is not broken down.

Among the new settlers were several who would play prominent roles in the coming drama. Joshua Webb was born in 1722 in Windham, Connecticut, a great-grandson of Governor William Bradford of Plymouth Colony. He married Hannah Abbe, with whom he had eleven children, the last two born in Westminster. Joshua Webb was Westminster's first schoolmaster, teaching in the log schoolhouse opposite Azariah Wright's house in 1765. In 1768, he moved to the northern part of Westminster and lived there from 1768 until 1777, when he moved to Rockingham.

Bildad Andros, born in 1719 in Southington, Connecticut, was a well-educated man and a skilled surgeon. When he settled in Northfield with his wife at age thirty-one in 1750, he was already a veteran of several skirmishes. He served in the army during the French and Indian War and took his oldest boy, Nathaniel, with him to camp at age nine to act as his assistant. In 1765, Andros took up land in Westminster, moving there in 1768. He favored New York and was politically active.

The West Parish was now filling up. The river valley lands had been taken up first; later, settlers and the second generation of East Parish settlers moved west. Divided by a series of steep hills rising from the Connecticut River Valley, the two parts of town feel farther apart than they actually are. Church attendance, family ties and, a little later, membership in Azariah Wright's militia drew people together frequently. Prominent among the West Parish families was Ephraim Wilcox, Silence Ranney's brother, who settled in the West Parish in 1761. Jabez Perry and his wife, Mary Ide, from Rehoboth, Massachusetts, built a log house in the southern part of the West Parish by 1762. Their daughter Polly was born that year, the first English child born in the West Parish. Mary's father and brothers soon joined the couple, taking up farms nearby.

The Crook brothers settled at the corner of present Patch Road in 1762. William Crook was twenty-six and a native of Haddam, Connecticut, where he acquired considerable schooling and worked on his father's farm. The French and Indian War broke out when he was seventeen. He joined the military at age twenty, and for the rest of his life he missed no opportunity for military service. He came to Westminster with his wife, Rebecca, and two sons, William Jr., a toddler, and the infant Ephraim. By 1768, William and Rebecca had been joined by William's brothers Andrew and Robert. Robert and his wife, Mercy, had three children by the end of 1771; William and Rebecca added another daughter that same year. A rushing brook known as Shim's Brook ran through their property, and they began building a sawmill and gristmill.

NEW YORK ACTION

Getting no action from the Crown, and watching New Hampshire sell its land out from under it, New York launched its own charter campaign. Direct physical conflict between New Hampshire grantees and New York survey teams began in western Cumberland County in 1769 and continued through the early 1770s, leading to the rise of Ethan Allen and the Green Mountain Boys. No such conflicts occurred in the Connecticut Valley. In Westminster, the settlers were busy establishing institutions, schools and, in 1767, a Congregational church, the third in present Vermont.

The conflict between the New England colonies and Great Britain now began to brush Westminster. A riot over impressments of sailors and the seizure of John Hancock's ship *Liberty* in 1768 led to Massachusetts being declared in a state of insurrection. Two British regiments were quartered in Boston. That same year, Azariah Wright established a "pure Whig" militia in Westminster, with himself as captain. The militia drilled at Wright's house on the Upper Street; Wright was remembered as a stern drillmaster. According to Hall, the policy of the Whigs prior to French's death "interdicted the use of fire arms." This could only refer to protest actions against government authorities; otherwise, the militia likely drilled with muskets in anticipation of renewed war against the Indians. (Note: Whig was the name the pro-independence group gave itself; New York government called it "the Mob.")

Members of Wright's militia were:

Captain Azariah Wright
Lieutenant Jabez Perry
First Sergeant Simeon Burke
Second Sergeant Jesse Burke

PRIVATES
Jacob Albee
John Albee
Lemuel Ames
Asa Averill
John Averill
Thomas Averill
Jabez Bates
Silas Burke
Atherton Chaffee
Andrew Crook
Robert Crook
William Crook
David Daley
Jonathan Fuller
Seth Goold
William Goold

Francis Holden
John Holt
Ichabod Ide
Israel Ide
Joseph Ide
Robert Miller
John Petty
Atwater Phippen
Joseph Phippen
Samuel Phippen
Robert Rand
James Richardson
Nathaniel Robertson (Robinson)
Reuben Robertson (Robinson)
Edmund Shipman
Jehiel Webb
John Wells[13]

This list seems to be based on local memory and not on a preserved roster. Hall asserts that "Liberty men" were few and far between in the East

The top of the Liberty Pole that stood near the courthouse in 1775. *Westminster Historical Society.*

Parish and that most who served under Azariah Wright on March 13 were from the West Parish, where the majority of inhabitants were Whigs. But a rough count shows at least fourteen East Parish men on this roll. Eight were certainly from the West Parish, and it's difficult to know the residence of the remaining fifteen. Membership was a family affair; there were three Phippens, three Burkes (also spelled Burk), three Ides, three Crooks, two Albees and two Goolds, but only one Wright, Captain Azariah. Azariah's closest neighbors on the Upper Street, Joel Holton, John Norton and his own brother Medad, were not members.

The idea that "Liberty men" were few and far between in the East Parish is false but is the flip side of an undeniable fact. All of Westminster's known New York sympathizers, and all of its Tories, lived in the East. If any in the West Parish harbored such sentiments, they kept their opinions well hidden. The West Parish was chiefly settled after the declaration of 1764 made it clear(ish) that the lands west of the Connecticut belonged to New York. Being on shaky legal ground may have helped firm up West Parish opinions. East Parish people had long experience of floating from colony to colony without disturbance to their property rights.

In 1769, Westminster's pastor, Jesse Goodell, fled abruptly after he was seen walking on the riverbank at twilight with a woman not his wife. He abandoned his wife and children; his brother-in-law collected them and moved them to Charlestown, New Hampshire.

THE DEAN INCIDENT

An incident relating to the Naval Stores Act touched Westminster in 1769. The Dean brothers, Willard and William, of Windsor, cut some pine trees that should have been reserved for the king's navy. Because the Deans were New York loyalists, Governor Wentworth prosecuted; he ignored this crime when committed by friends of New Hampshire. The Deans were arrested, threatened and bustled off to jail in the city of New York. They spent a night at Ephraim Ranney's inn in Westminster, where attorney John Grout met them and was able to get them kinder treatment. In Marlboro the next night, a mob beset the house where the men were being held but desisted when informed that the Deans were not being mistreated.

The issue was ultimately resolved through legal finesse, with the Deans transferring ownership of their goods to Judge Samuel Wells, so the fines and penalties imposed on them had no effect. This, along with the kidnapping of lawyer John Grout by a mob in 1770, was part of growing aggression against New York institutions and their supporters on the east side of the Green Mountains. Only three years earlier, people had petitioned for the courts to be established; now they seemed oppressive, especially since the ownership of so much property remained in doubt.

The pastor-less Westminster congregation built a meetinghouse in the center of the King's Highway, on a line with the present town hall. It was ready to use, though far from finished, in 1770. Several early settlers were also upgrading to frame houses; Medad Wright built a gambrel-roofed house in 1770, and around the same time John Norton put up the large gambrel-roofed building that would be known as the Tory Tavern. On the Lower Street, John Goold also had a tavern; his would become known as the Whig, or People's, Tavern. With Michael Gilson's, south of

The Westminster meetinghouse didn't yet have its steeple in 1775. It stood on stone pillars in the center of the King's Highway. *Westminster Historical Society.*

The Tory Tavern, where Sheriff Paterson's men drank and planned before the Massacre. The site is a cornfield today. *Westminster Historical Society.*

Still standing, the Red Farmhouse is an example of Westminster's gambrel-roofed taverns built in the 1770s. *Postcard, Westminster Historical Society.*

the village, and Ephraim Ranney's to the north, that gave Westminster at least four taverns.

In 1772, a Royal Navy schooner chasing smugglers ran aground in Rhode Island and was burned by the county sheriff. Crown efforts to bring the criminals to justice led Samuel Adams to create the first Committee of Correspondence to disseminate information quickly and to coordinate action. In Westminster, Dummerston and Rockingham, people like Azariah Wright and Reuben Jones began to connect to these groups.

The 1770s dawned in violence and disorder. In Boston, a mob snowballed the occupying redcoats, and the soldiers fired on them, killing five men and boys. In the Grants, the supposedly settled question of jurisdiction heated up again. Between 1769 and 1771, petitions flooded from eastern Vermont to the king and governors of New York and New Hampshire, attempting to push the Grants toward one colony or the other.

One such petition from November 1, 1770, bemoaned the disruption of the Chester court and the kidnapping of court officials by Nathan Stone, a New Hampshire adherent, and his friends. Of 432 signatures on this petition favoring stronger government by New York, 2 are from Westminster—Ephraim Wilcox and Nathan Goold. Other signers would, by 1775, be vehement opponents of New York, most notably Leonard Spaulding of Dummerston.

Another petition, circulated in several towns including Westminster from late 1768 to 1769, sought re-annexation to New Hampshire, an idea floated by Governor John Wentworth. It alleged numerous wrongs suffered by "Your Magesty's loyal, faithful obedient subjects":

> *Their possessions have been unexceptionally granted to other people under the great Seal of New York—that writs of ejectments have been brought, their property wrested from them, their persons Imprisoned and their whole substance wasted in fruitless Law Suits merely to the enrichment of a few Men in said Province of New York, whose great Influence is the distruction of our hard, honestly earned property, that we were greatly and industriously cultivating the wilderness…we are thrown in such evident distress confusion and dangerous disorder as would touch your Royal Breast with Compassn could our inexpressable Missery be Truly represented.*

This petition was promoted in Westminster by Benjamin Burt, who five years later would be an active supporter of New York. It was signed by fifty-six Westminster citizens:

William Willard Esquire
William Willard Jr.
Joseph Willard
James Richardson
John Patterson
Benjamin Burt
John Avery (Averill)
John Avery Jr. (Averill)
Samuel C. Avery (Averill)
Joseph Phippney (Phippen?)
Joseph Stoddard
Jonathan Burk
Jesse Burk
So. Burke
Amos Carpenter Jr.
Eleazer Harlough (Harlow)
Jacop Abby
James Crafford (Crawford?)
Silas Burk
John Petty
Ephram Spencer
John Sessions
   Gilson (Michael?)
William Heaton
Zakariah Gilson
Jonathan Gilson
Joseph Arwin
Abial Gooddale (Goodell?)
Caleb Spencer

William Hill
Gidion Bagger (Badger?)
Thomas Davis
Thomas Davis Jr.
Charles Crook
Levy Androes
Bridges Medcalf (Metcalf)
Charles Holding (Holden)
Simeon Burk
   Wright (Azariah?)
   Dickinson
Medad Wright
Joel Holton
Samuel Cone
Asa Averel (Averill)
Isaac Patterson
Benjamin Patterson
Michael Metcalf
Bildad Andros Esq.
Amas Carpenter
   Carpenter
   Carpenter
Timothy Carpenter
Jidiah Prior
Andrew Crook
Abel Carpenter
   Webb
John Goold[14]

At least eight signers would be energetically on the side of New York five years later: William Willard, William Willard Jr., Joseph Willard, Benjamin Burt, Bildad Andros, Medad Wright, John Sessions and Michael Gilson. Other Westminster signers include four members of his militia and probably Azariah himself.

The re-annexation petition made allegations that are fairly eye-popping. Ejectments? Imprisonments? In Westminster? Reading closely, we note that the petition didn't say where these events occurred. If the king wished to infer that oppressive conditions existed all over the Grants, he was free to do so.

A number of prominent men organized to rebut the re-annexation petition, including Oliver Willard, brother-in-law of William and uncle of William Jr. and Joseph; Judge Samuel Wells (Brattleboro); and John Kelly (New York City; law partner of Crean Brush). In depositions before Daniel Horsmanden, chief justice of the province of New York in late February and early March 1771, they alleged that the re-annexation petitions were promoted and perhaps even written by Governor Wentworth. They said they'd never heard of any ejectments east of the Green Mountains and claimed to know of no settlers who were soldiers in His Majesty's Regular Forces, only one or two deserters and a few rangers. (A claim of the petition was that many of them had been soldiers in the French and Indian War. In fact, several Westminster settlers were former soldiers in that war; William Crook was certainly a member of the regular army.) They also charged that the signatures of underage youth were actively sought. Certainly Joseph Willard was only eleven or twelve when he signed.

Few Brattleboro or Guilford citizens signed, Wells said, "as they are almost universally desirous of remaining in the Province of New York." He was "convinced that of the whole Inhabitants of the Counties of Cumberland and Gloucester a great majority are desirous of remaining within the Jurisdiction of the Government of New York, the strength of the opposition thereto laying in the Townships of Windsor Newbury and Westminster, and among some scattered Inhabitants in some few other Towns."[15]

The re-annexation petition might have been exaggerated, but conditions in Westminster and eastern Cumberland County were bad enough. Many settlers were in debt, crops were uncertain and the troubles with Britain had caused an economic depression. According to Chilton Williamson, "The surviving records of the Cumberland County Court of Common Pleas consist largely of suits for the recovery of debts."[16]

Chapter 2
"Our Just Rights"

CREAN BRUSH

Into this situation stepped the Irish Loyalist politician Crean Brush, bent on making his name and fortune. Brush, an ambitious attorney with many friends in New York government, moved to Westminster in 1771. The events of the next four years can't be understood without some idea of who and what this new citizen was.

The Brush family had been loyal to the Crown since Crean's great-grandfather, John Brush (1665–1741), was an officer in a Dutch regiment fighting the Irish Jacobites at the Battle of the Boyne. The family received land as reward, and Crane Brush was born on the estate of Darkmany in Omagh in 1727. He received a military commission and was familiarly called "Colonel"; he trained for and practiced law in Ireland. Around the age of thirty, he married and had a child, Elizabeth Martha, born in 1758. Mrs. Brush died in childbirth. Crane left Elizabeth in the care of relatives and came to America around 1762.

He settled in New York City, changed his name to Crean and rapidly found employment with the province of New York. For several years he was assistant to the deputy secretary of the province, Goldsbrow Banyar. He received his license to practice law in New York from Cadwallader Colden in 1764 and became John Kelly's law partner. Kelly, like Brush, was a land speculator.[17]

Crean Brush as a young man. The Tory lawyer brought Westminster to prominence in the early 1770s. *From History of Eastern Vermont, by Benjamin H. Hall.*

THE BRUSH WOMEN

In 1762, Brush married Margaret Schoolcraft, oldest daughter of English soldier James Schoolcraft, at the Albany home of Colonel John Bradstreet. Margaret was already the guardian or mother of a little girl, Frances, the future Fanny Allen.

Fanny's exact parentage is obscure. In the 1850s, when Benjamin Hall was writing *The History of Eastern Vermont*, the story was that she was Margaret's daughter by a former marriage to a British officer; supposedly Crean Brush had courted Margaret early in life, but she had chosen the officer, who died in battle. But no such marriage has been found, and apparently this story was never told until 1851.[18] Its timing is problematic on several fronts.

Circumstantial evidence and family lore suggest that Fanny was actually Margaret's niece. Her mother, Margaret's younger sister, was the underage

Margaret Schoolcraft married Crean Brush, supported him loyally and even broke him out of jail. With her second husband, Patrick Wall, she lived for many years in Westminster. *Copyright Fort Ticonderoga Museum; used by permission.*

Fanny Montusan, illegitimate daughter of a British officer, was raised by Crean Brush. As a young widow, she married Ethan Allen in Stephen Bradley's Westminster home. *Copyright Fort Ticonderoga Museum; used by permission.*

mistress of John Montresor, a noted British officer. Fanny's mother died shortly after giving birth; by that time, Montresor had deserted them, and Margaret became Fanny's guardian. Margaret has been described as the widow Montusan (many versions of the name were current), but she was never married to a Montresor or anyone else. The circumstance of Fanny's birth was described in the extremely popular American novel *Charlotte Temple*, written by a cousin of John Montresor.[19]

Brush moved to Westminster about 1771. According to Hall, coming to Vermont gave him an opportunity to sell his lands; he had received ten thousand acres in Bennington from Cadwallader Colden. "He also hoped to rise in political distinction, an end which he could not hope to accomplish among the learned and aristocratic in the more southern towns of New York."

Brush brought his wife and twelve-year-old stepdaughter to Westminster, and the family moved into the house that had been built for Reverend Goodell only two years before. It stood kitty-corner to the street, its sides each facing one of the cardinal directions, the only house in Westminster with that orientation.

According to Hall, Brush brought a clerk with him, Abraham Mills,

> *who, as far as disagreeable traits of character were concerned, was a copy in miniature of his master...On becoming a resident of Westminster, Mr. Brush was feasted by the inhabitants from house to house. The display which he affected in his dress, contrasted strongly with the simple garb of the visitors, and for some time pomp and parade availed to conceal the defects of character. But as vulgarity of mind became apparent, and novelty of appearance ceased to attract, Mr. Brush found, in spite of his boasted attainments as a man of large information, and his pretensions to gentility, that his only friends were a few hightoned and arrogant loyalists.*

(And Atherton Chaffee, a member of the Whig militia; Chaffee's last, posthumous son was named Crean Brush Chaffee.)

Hall may be accused of having twenty-twenty hindsight, but Brush's contemporaries also spoke ill of him. One colleague in the New York Assembly called him "a stupid fellow." In those days, stupid meant uncouth as well as lacking in intellect. The Patriot Ebenezer Hazard noticed Brush's "sharp nose...his face is full of red or crimson pimples, like a drunkard's."[20]

Lack of widespread popularity didn't hold Brush back. "Mr. Brush wielded an extensive political influence in the county, on account of his intimate connection with many of the principal government officers."[21] For a few years, the weight of this powerful man bent Westminster history around him.

In 1771, the courthouse and jail in Chester provided by Judge Thomas Chandler were unfinished and so unsatisfactory that when Atherton Chaffee was imprisoned there, he told an official "that he knew it was out of Whipple's [the sheriff's] power to confine him against his will but that Whipple had always used him with great tenderness, and that he should not be hurt; for, says Chaffee, I will tarry in the jail be it never so slender—rather than Whipple should be hurt."[22]

Chester was the geographic but not the population center of Cumberland County. From 1771, coinciding with the arrival of Crean Brush, southern Cumberland County towns began jostling to become the shire town. Chandler fought back, making overblown claims about Chester's roads, courthouse and jail and arguing that its very out-of-the-way location made Chester safer, as mobs were less likely to go there and break prisoners out of jail.

Crean Brush contrived to get John Chandler removed as clerk of Cumberland County and himself appointed on February 25, 1772. Two days later, on February 27, a petition requesting that the courts be moved to Westminster was read to the New York House of Representatives. A bill allowing the county to vote on the shire town was passed on March 24.

Westminster still operated under the 1760 New Hampshire charter. This would not do for the shire town of a New York county. On March 26, 1772, New York issued a new Westminster charter "to certain grantees who conveyed to Col. Josiah Willard, then of Winchester, N.H., and he executed releases to such of the former proprietors, or their assigns, as chose to take titles under the new authority."[23]

A series of meetings of the county supervisors followed, and on May 19 they chose Westminster as the shire town and voted to build a courthouse and jail there.

COURT, JAIL AND TAVERN

Originally, the Cumberland County Courthouse was intended to adjoin the public street as near as possible to the meetinghouse. At a June 11 meeting, that decision was reversed by a majority of one, and a new site was voted near present Westminster Station. Crean Brush reported this decision to Governor Tryon, with the slant that the reversal of the first decision had been "inadvertently acquiesced in" by some members of the board of

We Ephraim Ranny, Benjamin Burt, and John Norton Persons appointed to Superintend the Building of the Court House and Goal in the Township of Westminster in and for the County of Cumberland, and to Carry into Execution the Determination of the Supervisors of the said County at their meeting held at Chester on the twenty sixth Day of May last and the Order of his Excellency the Governor and Council conforming the same, Do pursuant to the Authority by the said Order given to us, hereby Certify and Declare that after mature consideration We have unanimously agreed that the said Court House and Goal shall be erected and Built about eighty Rods to the Northward of the meeting House in the said Township of Westminster on the East side of the Common Highway or Path as the same is now Travelled to the Westward of the House Lotts Number Sixty one and Number Sixty two opposite to the division Line between

between the said Lotts about Twenty feet of the said building to be to the Northward of the said division Line, and twenty feet thereof to be to the Southward of the said division Line Given under our Hands at Westminster this Eleventh Day of September One thousand Seven hundred and Seventy two.

Ephraim Ranney
Benjamin Burt
John Norton

This page: Crean Brush engineered Westminster's ascension to shire town of Cumberland County. This document authorized the building of the courthouse in 1772. *Westminster Historical Society.*

supervisors who now were convinced of the impropriety of this act. We have only Brush's word that anyone repented of the second vote, but acting on his information, the governor and council approved the first site, which was only a few hundred yards from Brush's own house.[24]

> *There was still standing on this plain considerable of the original forest. There were then on the plain where the village now stands some 12 or 15 dwellings, and nearly as many on the upper street. The Court House... stood in the middle of the highway, on the top of what we call the Court House hill. Were it now standing a considerable part of it would project over where the embankment is broken off, on your right as you descend the hill, and be a few paces this side of the spring.*[25]

The Westminster Courthouse occupied a commanding location, a fit setting for the dramas that would take place there.

> *In shape it was almost square, the sides being about forty feet in length, and was built of hewn timber, clap-boarded. The roof was gambrel, surmounted by a cupola or tower, open at the four sides. An aisle, ten or twelve feet in width, ran east and west through the middle of the lower story. A double door was placed at each end of the aisle, or, in other words, two doors opening either way from a center fastening. In accordance with*

Charles Jo Brasor (1865–1930) made this drawing of the Westminster Courthouse in 1929. Brasor was a native of Brattleboro and spent much of his artistic career in New York. This drawing was among many found in the attic of the old Brasor house many years after his death and is currently owned by Richard Michelman.

Interior of the courthouse. Upper left is the courtroom; upper right is the jailer's quarters. Below is the barroom; through the doorways and across the corridor are the cells. *Scale model by Dorothy Metros, 1976, Westminster Historical Society.*

The courthouse barroom served the judges and lawyers, probably the Whigs who occupied the courthouse and certainly the already well-lit sheriff's party after the massacre. *Metros model, Westminster Historical Society.*

the custom of the times, the building was intended to afford some of the conveniences of a tavern. In the south-east corner was a kitchen or cook-room, occupied by the jailer, and in the south-west corner, a bar-room, in which the jailer served in the capacity of a bar-tender. The chimney rose between these rooms, and opened into each in the shape of a large old-fashioned fire-place. Another door was cut in the south side of the building, leading into an entry, on either side of which were doors to the kitchen and bar-room.

In the north part was the jail, which comprised within its limits two prison-rooms, divided the one from the other by a narrow aisle running north and south. This aisle communicated with the broad aisle, by a door. Doors also opened from the prison-rooms into the narrow aisle. A flight of stairs led from the east entrance to the court-room in the second story. [26]

Westminster, shire town, consisted of four taverns and possibly twenty-five houses and log cabins on the Upper and Lower Streets, with barns and outbuildings. The church, newly finished and without a steeple, perched in the middle of the Lower Street on stone pillars. Dogs, pigs, horses and cattle added noise, liveliness and manure to the street. Margaret Brush and Fanny Montusan added elegance and New York glamour, and Crean Brush added political importance.

The new courthouse wasn't the only change happening in Westminster. By the fall of 1772, Brush was literally redrawing the map. A map held in the Vermont State Archives shows Westminster lots and their owners. Though dated 1774, it bears the following inscription:

County of Cumberland Clerks Office 19th Sept 1774
The Above Plan is a True Copy of a Certain Plan annexed to a Certain Deed from Josiah Willard Esquire To Crean Brush bearing Date the Twenty Third Day of September in the Year of our Lord One Thousand Seven Hundred and Seventy Two and Recorded in the office at the Desire of the said Crean Brush and the Inhabitants of the Township of Westminster.
S. Gale, Clk.

Josiah Willard appears to have transferred thousands of acres in Westminster to Mr. Brush: 3,340 by my count, most in 80- and 100-acre lots in the western part of town. In addition, Brush owned two house lots on the Lower Street. Willard's name appears nowhere on this map.

The precise connection between Westminster becoming the shire town, Willard receiving the renewal of the Westminster charter from New York and Brush buying all his lands (and succeeding him as the most important Westminster citizen) can only be speculated on. Brush was good at making things happen, and once he arrived in Westminster, more things happened here than ever before.

William Paterson (sometimes spelled Patterson), born in Ireland of Scotch-Irish descent, was a friend of Crean Brush and joined him in Westminster in 1772 or 1773. Sheriff Daniel Whipple was liked by Judge Chandler, but Samuel Wells and Noah Sabin, associate judges with Chandler, lobbied Governor Tryon to have him removed, accusing him of corruption and negligence. Their statements were corroborated by Crean Brush. Whipple was removed from office and Paterson put in his place. Paterson's place of residence is variously given as Westminster, Hinsdale, Brattleboro or Fulham (Dummerston).

In December 1772, citizens of Cumberland County wrote to Governor Tryon requesting the right to elect a representative to the New York General Assembly. Westminster signers included William Willard, Bildad Andros, Crean Brush, Ephraim Ranney and John Norton. Permission to elect two representatives was granted. Brush and Samuel Wells, both Yorkers and Tories, were elected to the General Assembly.

This may have been a rigged election. Hall cites a note written to Wells by John Bolton, "who was probably a successful wire-puller,"[27] dated at Westminster, June 11, 1773. "Sir: I have paid unto Jont. Safford nine Shillings and Six pence Lawful money of the Bay Province, for Necesares the People of Halifax had when they Come to Lextion if you wold be so good as to pay y(e) same to Mr. Whipple y(e) Bearer by next thursday so as he may bring it to me, you will much oblige your Humble Servt."[28]

Brush resigned as county clerk on March 7, 1774, and was succeeded by Samuel Gale, Samuel Wells's son-in-law. The *Connecticut Courant*, in listing the members of the last Colonial Assembly of New York, noted of Brush, "A native of Ireland, practising the law in Cumberland county, who sold the clerkship of the county to Judge Wells's son-in-law."[29] Brush was with the New York Assembly in time to vote on the so-called Bloody Act, an antiriot law aimed at Ethan Allen and the Green Mountain Boys. It made those guilty of unlawful assembly liable to a year in prison and made members of a mob who refused an official order to disperse liable to the death penalty.[30]

In his three brief years in Westminster, Crean Brush had made his hometown the county seat, replaced the county sheriff with his own crony, subverted the vote of the county supervisors and relocated the courthouse closer to his own home, gotten his county two seats in the assembly and engineered an election to take one of those seats for himself. He had also helped set up the conditions under which a peaceful protest in Westminster would turn deadly.

Brush although in a great measure devoid of principle, possessed many of the qualifications essential to the character of a successful partizan politician, and he soon became noted for his advocacy of all ministerial measures, and for his hatred of every attempt at reform. Fluency of speech and a spirited style of oratory, enabled him to give expression to his opinions in a manner which attracted attention. By these means he obtained an influence, which he never failed to exert in behalf of his party. In the controversy between New Hampshire and New York respecting the New Hampshire Grants, he evinced a deep interest, and was well prepared by knowledge obtained while in the office of the secretary of state to present the question in an accurate and reliable form.[31]

MASSACHUSETTS FARMERS' REVOLUTION

While the upheaval in the western grants held New York's attention, Massachusetts experienced a mass movement that was a direct precursor to the Westminster Massacre. In 1773, following the Boston Tea Party, Parliament enacted the Coercive Acts, closing the port of Boston and taking over elective government. All judges and representatives were now appointed by the Crown. General Thomas Gage was appointed both royal governor of Massachusetts and commander in chief of British forces in the colonies, creating a military government. In 1774, Gage moved the colonial capital to Salem.

The Coercive Acts had limited town meetings to one per year. Salem convened an illegal meeting in late August 1774 right under General Gage's nose. When Gage marched two companies of the Fifty-ninth Regiment to the site, they were faced down by a large number of farmers. When Gage later tried to arrest members of the local Committee of Correspondence, three thousand men assembled to rescue them, and Gage backed down.

Through late August and early September, enormous crowds forced the courts in Worcester, Great Barrington, Plymouth, Concord, Northampton, Springfield and Taunton (Westminster's parent town) to close. In Worcester, five to six thousand men showed up to prevent the court from opening. Later, two to three thousand visited Crown-appointed councilor Timothy Paine at his home and forced his resignation.

Most of these actions were nonviolent, but they must have been terrifying to the agents of the Crown and exhilarating to the farmers who had essentially overturned Crown rule in Massachusetts. Their cousins and former neighbors in Westminster would have paid close attention. Citizens who felt that New York courts had been imposed on them would have drawn a direct comparison, and perhaps an object lesson, from Worcester, Northampton and Taunton.[32]

ISAAC LOW'S LETTER

Isaac Low, a New York City merchant and leading Whig, was appointed chairman of the New York Committee of Correspondence in May 1774. Two days before his appointment, on May 21, he wrote a letter to the Cumberland County supervisors asking about the sentiments of the people regarding the previous year's events in Massachusetts. The supervisors met in June but took no action on Low's letter and attempted to conceal its existence.

But it was hard to keep a secret in Cumberland County. Somehow Azariah Wright and Reuben Jones of Rockingham, both staunch Whigs, got wind of the letter and notified their towns. Committees from Westminster and Rockingham confronted the supervisors at their September meeting, wondering "whether any papers had been received which ought to be laid before the several towns of the county."[33]

The supervisors then produced Low's letter and had a copy sent to each town. A county convention was called to meet on October 19 at Westminster to decide what action to take.

FIRST WESTMINSTER CONVENTION

The Westminster Convention of October 19–20, 1774, was the first held in Vermont to oppose the pressure from Great Britain. Westminster's representative was Joshua Webb, the schoolmaster. He was on the committee that studied the relevant documents: Low's letter, the act of Parliament levying a tax on tea, the bill that closed the port of Boston and other declarations of the British government.

The committee reported on the second day of the two-day convention. It reviewed the sufferings of the pioneers and argued strongly against the acts of Parliament:

> *He who has nothing but what another has power at pleasure lawfully to take away from him, has nothing that he can call his own, and is, in the fullest sense of the word, as slave…and as no part of British America stipulated to settle as slaves, the privileges of British subjects are their privileges, and whoever endeavours to deprive them of their privileges is guilty of treason against the Americans, as well as the British constitution.*

They were not yet revolutionary. They were arguing for their rights as British subjects, and the resolutions of the First Convention expressed loyalty both to the king and to their own rights:

> *As true and loyal subjects of our gracious sovereign, King George the Third of Great Britain…we will spend our lives and fortunes in his service; that as we will defend our King while he reigns over us…and wish his reign may be long and glorious, so we will defend our just rights, as British subjects, against every power that shall attempt to deprive us of them, while breath is in our nostrils and blood in our veins.*

The resolution condemned the recent acts of Parliament as arbitrary, and "be it right or wrong, we resolve to assist the people of Boston in defense of their liberties to the utmost of our abilities."

The Whigs seem to have had a policy of nonviolence. Evidence of this determination is the wording of the resolution passed at the First Convention at Westminster:

> *Sensible that the strength of our opposition to the late acts consists in a uniform, manly, steady, and determined mode of procedure, we will bear testimony against and discourage all riotous, tumultuous, and unnecessary mobs which tend to injure the persons or properties of harmless individuals; but endeavour to treat those persons whose abominable principles and actions show them to be enemies to American liberty, as loathsome animals not fit to be touched or have any society or connection with.*[34]

It sounds a bit like grade school shunning—Tories have cooties!—but this resolution is also strongly nonviolent and shows a sense of dignity.

A committee was set up to communicate with other Committees of Correspondence. Of the five members, two were from Westminster: Joshua Webb and John Sessions. A letter was drafted to Isaac Low, but for some reason the results of the convention weren't published until the next year, causing a rumor that Cumberland County was unfriendly to the Continental Congress.

Nothing could have been further from the case, but not until June 23, more than two months after the Westminster Massacre, did a letter to the editor in the *New York Journal* make this clear. This letter, probably written by John Hazeltine, the chairman of the convention, concludes, "The long delay of the publication was occasioned by some unfair practices of a small but mischievous party, together with the remote situation of the County from the City of New York."[35]

We have no idea who caused this delay. Cumberland County was divided into factions, and control of information was crucial. The two sides kept a close eye on each other, intercepting letters in some cases and withholding them in others. The flow of information suggests that there was someone friendly to Whig interests within court circles and vice versa.

ARTICLES OF ASSOCIATION

In 1774, the Continental Congress had not yet declared independence but was leaning in that direction. On October 20, it adopted the Non-Importation, Non-Consumption and Non-Exportation Association, attempting to cut off all trade with Britain. The New York General Assembly rejected the association, the only colony to do so.

But at a convention at Westminster on November 30, Cumberland County voted to "religiously adhere to" the association's provisions. (The convention was laughed down when it attempted to choose a Committee of Inspection to "attentively...observe the conduct of all persons." This Big Brother–like committee would have watched for signs of Tory sympathizing and taken action against them. A committee was voted in Dummerston, and later they were active in many towns, but in November 1774 men of standing in Cumberland County were able to make the majority of delegates feel that an action like this was preposterous.)[36] Cumberland County had adopted the Articles of Association; the province of New York had not. What was the county to do? It was now in violation of the Fourteenth Article, by which it had resolved to have "no trade, commerce, dealings, or intercourse whatsoever, with any colony or province in North America" that did not accept the association. It had promised to hold violators of the association "as unworthy of the rights of freemen, and as inimical to the liberties of their country." Those enemies of freedom were the very people who ran Cumberland County and ruled on all cases of debt.

There were many such cases. According to the Whig committee that investigated the Massacre, the Tories knew "that there was no cash stirring, and they took that opportunity to collect debts, knowing that men had no other way to pay them than by having their estates taken by execution and sold at vendue."[37] There were many lawsuits and imprisoned debtors.

SPAULDING JAILED AND SPRUNG

King George caused concern in the American colonies with the Quebec Act, which established the Roman Catholic religion in Quebec rather than merely tolerating it, as the Crown had earlier. Residents of Quebec were deprived of the right of assembly. Trials by jury and the English laws were abolished, and the laws of France were established in their place, "in direct violation," says Hall, "of his Majesty's promise in his royal proclamation."[38]

These actions raised eyebrows in New England, where there had been recent bitter fighting against the French in Quebec and where there was strong feeling against the Catholic Church. What was the point of all that bloodshed if the Quebecois were not to be turned into Englishmen? Dummerston resident Leonard Spaulding's crime was to comment that "if the king had signed the Quebec bill, it was his opinion that he had broke his coronation-oath."[39]

According to Solomon Harvey, also of Dummerston, Spaulding was arrested "by the direction of the infamous Crean Brush...& Noah Sabin, William Willard, and Ephraim Ranney Esqrs., and Wm. Paterson the high Shreeve, and Benja. Gorton, and the infamous Bildad Easton, and his Deputies."

It took several men to arrest Spaulding, "a resolute man." He languished in jail for eleven days, until a party of his neighbors, assisted by large groups from Putney, Guilford, Halifax and Draper (now Wilmington), broke him out of the Westminster jail on November 8. The exact method they used is left vague. Harvey says only that they "opened the goal [In official and unofficial writings of the time, gaol (jail) was frequently spelled as "goal."] without Key or Lock-picker, and after Congratulating Mr. Spaulding upon the recovery of his freedom, Dispersed Every man in pease to his respective home or place of abode."[40]

THIRD WESTMINSTER CONVENTION

Held February 7–9, 1775, this convention dealt primarily with local issues and seems to have been conducted in taverns. On the first day, the meeting "adjourned to Mr Nortons at Seven o clock this Evening," Mr. Norton's being the Tory Tavern. This session was "Adjorn[d] to Deacon Ranneys to meet tomorrow morning Eight o clock." Deacon Ranney also had a tavern. The courthouse was also equipped with a kitchen and bar, but it was February, and possibly the Norton and Ranney taverns were warmer.

Joshua Webb and Abijah Lovejoy of Westminster were named to a five-person group to "Serve as Monitors to the Committee of correspondance to transfer All letters & other Matters that are of Consequence or inteligence to the chareman, Co(l) Hazelton."[41] This was an important job; already the results of an earlier convention had not been handled properly, and other information would go astray as well.

The Cumberland County Courthouse was the preeminent symbol of Westminster's importance and the scene of crucial events like Vermont's declaration of independence. *Vermont, the Green Mountain State,* Walter Hill Crockett.

"TIME TO LOOK TO THEMSELVES"

The Whigs knew they couldn't trust their own government. The county council had concealed Isaac Low's letter from them last summer. Now the council blew hot and cold on the resolutions of the Westminster meeting. The Committee of Investigation report on the Massacre, dated March 23, 1775, put it this way:

> *Our men in office would say that they did like the resolutions of the continental congress, and they ought to be strictly adhered to until our general assembly voted against them. Then they said, that this would do for the Bay-Province, but that it was childish for us to pay any regard to them. Some of our court would boldly say, that the King had a just right to make the revenue acts, for he had a supreme power, and he that said otherwise was guilty of high treason, and they did hope that they would be executed accordingly.*[42]

With the New York provincial authorities and Cumberland County officials in violation of the agreement the colonies had just made, the Whigs feared—or said they feared—an economic embargo against them. New York deserved one. Cumberland County did not. And they had strong reason to distrust all levels of government.

> *The people were of opinion that such men were not suitable to rule over them; and as the general assembly of this Province would not accede to the association of the continental congress, the good people were of opinion, that if they did accede to any power from or under them, they should be guilty of the breach of the 14th article of that association, and may be justly dealt with, accordingly, by all America. When the good people considered that the general assembly were for bringing them into a state of slavery (which did appear plain by their not acceding to the best method to procure their liberties, and the executive power so strongly acquiescing in all that they did, whether it was right or wrong), the good people of said county thought it was time to look to themselves.*[43]

These words were written by Rockingham's Dr. Reuben Jones, clerk of the committee, on March 23, 1775, ten days after the Massacre. Lexington and Concord hadn't happened yet, let alone the Declaration of Independence. No one knew what was coming. No one knew that the views expressed in this report would be ratified by history. Those questioning the divine right of kings might yet be hanged, as Cumberland County Tories seemed to hope.

Yet the tone was calm, firm, convinced; the people were "the good people," and their decisions and deliberations were presented as rational and just. They were writing about themselves, of course (Jones was a participant in the Massacre and its aftermath). But the reasoned tone of the report says much about how they saw themselves and how they wanted to be seen by the world at large; not as rabble-rousers but as firm, fair, just and temperate. They had voted certain actions that their government wasn't ready to fall in with. What were they to do? It seemed to many that allowing the court to sit, and submitting to its decrees, would make Cumberland County complicit in New York's action.

> *And they thought it was dangerous to trust their lives and fortunes in the hands of such enemies to American liberty; but more particularly unreasonable that there should be any court held, since thereby we must accede to what our general assembly had done, in not acceding to what the whole continent had recommended; and that all America would break off all dealings and commerce with us, and bring us into a state of slavery at once. Therefore in duty to GOD, ourselves and posterity, we thought ourselves under the strongest obligation to resist and to oppose all authority that would not accede to the resolves of the continental congress. But knowing that many of our court were men that neither feared nor regarded men, we thought that it was most prudent to go and persuade the judges to stay at home.*[44]

Chapter 3
"Red Westminster"

A Little Visit

"Anxious to free themselves from the charges of haste and rashness," Hall says, "and to proceed as peaceably as possible, they deemed it prudent to request the judges to stay at home." As a revolutionary act, this visit—though doubtless intended to be intimidating—was an extremely polite one.

The impetus for visiting the judges came from Rockingham. Judge Wells was in New York at the assembly. The obvious judge to visit was Chandler in nearby Chester. All other courts in the region had been stopped by this time. The March 14 session of the court of common pleas at Westminster was the last scheduled.

On Friday, March 10, the Rockingham men paid a visit to Chandler.

Accordingly there were about forty good, true men sent from Rockingham to Chester, to dissuade Colonel Chandler, the chief judge, from attending court. He said he believed it would be for the good of the county not to have any court, as things were; but there was one case of murder that they must see to, and if it was not agreeable to the people, they would not have any other case. One of the committee told him that the sheriff would raise a number with arms, and that there would be bloodshed. The Colonel said that he would give his word and honor that there should not be any arms brought against us, and he would go down to court on Monday, the 13th of March inst., which was the day that the court was to be opened. We told him that we would wait on him, if it was his will. He said, that our company would be very agreeable; likewise he returned us his hearty thanks for our civility, and so we parted with him.[45]

If Chandler's response seemed too good to be true to the departing forty, they were right. Chandler immediately wrote to his fellow judges, who received word of the visitation later that same day.

A Posse Gathers

Chandler may have wished to be loyal to his king without the people being harmed. Other court officials, such as Noah Sabin and Samuel Gale, cared much more for the king than for their rebellious neighbors. They were determined that the court sit, and Chandler gave in to them. Sabin and others in Brattleboro alerted Sheriff William Paterson and made plans to occupy the courthouse and preserve the peace.

Messengers must have been racing up and down the frozen dirt roads. The same day as their visit to Chester, word of the court party's plans reached the Whigs.

> *We heard from the southern part of the state, that Judge Sabin was very earnest to have the law go on, as well as many petty officers…There was a great deal of talk in what manner to stop the court; and at length it was agreed on to let the court come together, and lay the reasons we had against their proceeding, before them, thinking they were men of such sense that they would hear them. But on Friday we heard that the court was going to take possession of the house on the 13th inst., and to keep a strong guard at the doors of said house, that we could not come in. We being justly alarmed by the deceit of our court, though it was not strange, therefore we thought proper to get to the court before the armed guards were placed; for we were determined that our grievances should be laid before the court, before it was opened.*[46]

We don't know how the Whigs received word of the court's plan. Possibly there was a spy within the Yorkist government, perhaps the same person who leaked word of Isaac Low's letter the year before.

Thomas Chandler Jr. may have been involved. He lived in Chester, was a friend of independence and is said by Azariah Wright to have written a letter "to Incurrige the ferse Soons of Liberty to assembel att Westminster,

Declaring he new his farthers mind." Chandler's letter was later interpreted by Wright as a trap; the fierce Sons of Liberty did assemble at Westminster and were mowed down. If the younger Chandler did write such a letter, his faith in his father's powers of persuasion was misplaced. But the letter, if it ever existed, is lost to us and may have had nothing to do with the leak of the Tory plans.

Sheriff Paterson spent Sunday gathering about twenty-five men from Brattleboro to help him secure the courthouse. On Monday, March 13, they marched north to Westminster. Paterson's men were armed only with clubs, but on the road they were joined by others, including about fourteen men with rifles. Paterson apparently did not encourage these men to leave their firearms at home.

Among the Whigs, in contrast, according to Theophilus Crawford (a child of eight at the time), "a man named Gates, of Dummerston, started for Westminster armed with a sword," and "the people would not let him proceed until he had laid aside the offensive weapon."[47]

The same day, March 13, about forty men from Chester and Rockingham marched to Westminster. Others came from Brattleboro and Dummerston. The Chester men got a send-off from Thomas Chandler Jr., who stated his opinions forthrightly: "The attorneys vexed the People with a

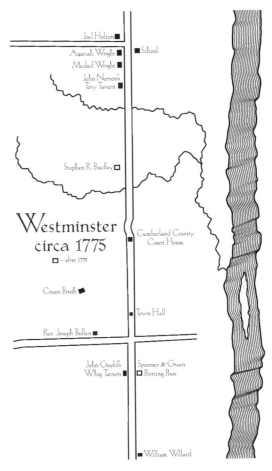

Important sites in 1770s Westminster. The road north of Courthouse Hill was known as the Upper Street, though it is lower in elevation than the Lower Street, south of Courthouse Hill. *Martha Haas, from Beers's 1869 Atlas.*

multiplicity of suits." The "sheriff of the County was undeserving to hold his office" and "had bad men for his deputies." While he didn't join the marchers, the younger Chandler wished them every success.[48]

The marchers converged at the home of Captain Azariah Wright, where they were joined by men from Westminster. Wright's log cabin being too small to hold them, they adjourned to the log schoolhouse across the street and consulted about strategy. Then they marched on, pausing only to arm themselves with staves from Wright's woodpile.

Confrontation

On Monday, the 13th of March inst., there were about 100 of us entered the court house, about four o'clock in the afternoon. But we had but just entered, before we were alarmed by a large number of men, armed with guns, swords and pistols. But we, in the house, had not any weapons of war among us, and were determined that they should not come in with their weapons of war, except by the force of them.

Esquire Patterson came up at the head of his armed company, within about five yards of the door, and commanded us to disperse, to which he got no answer. [What Jones describes as "no answer" the court party the next day described as "threats and Menaces."] *He then caused the King's proclamation to be read, and told us, that if we did not disperse in fifteen minutes, "by God, he would blow a lane through us." We told them that they might come in, if they would unarm themselves, but not without.*

One of our men went out at the door, and asked them if they were come for war; told them that we were come for peace, and that we should be glad to hold a parley with them. At that Mr. Gale, the clerk of the court, drew a pistol, held it up, and said: "Damn the parley with such damn rascals as you are; I will hold no parley with such damn rascals, but by this,"— holding up his pistol. They gave us very harsh language, told us we should be in hell before morning; but after a while, they drew off a little from the house, and seemed to be in a consultation. Three of us went out to treat with them; but the most, or all we could get from them, was, that they would not talk with "such damned rascals as we were;" and we soon returned to the house, and they soon went off.[49]

Again, this sounds a trifle calmer in the committee report than it may have been in real life. A furious argument is reported to have followed

The key to the Cumberland County Courthouse. *Loaned by Dr. Joslin to Westminster Institute; Westminster Historical Society.*

Gale's remarks. The Tories told the "rioters" that they'd be in hell before morning. Charles Davenport of Dummerston replied that if the sheriff tried to take the courthouse, the Whigs would send him and all his men to hell in fifteen minutes.

It was about seven o'clock when Chandler arrived; the man who confronted him on his broken promise was Azariah Wright.

> *Colonel Chandler came in, and we laid the case before him, and told him that we had his word that there should not be any arms brought against us. He said that the arms were brought without his consent, but he would go and take them away from them, and we should enjoy the house undisturbed until morning, and that the court should come in the morning without arms, and should hear what we had to lay before them; and then he went away.*[50]

Chandler didn't keep his second promise either. The sheriff's posse was not disarmed, and there is no indication that Chandler ever tried. But the men inside the courthouse half believed him. They held a meeting, drew up a white paper and then most went off to find supper and a bed. "We then went out of the house and chose a committee, which drew up articles to stand for, and read them to the company; and they were voted nem. con. dic., and some of our men went to the neighbors, and as many as the court and their party saw, they bound."[51]

This account of Whigs being captured as they went around the neighborhood that evening is not told in other accounts. If true, it shows that the sheriff and Chandler continued to act in bad faith.

The Whigs weren't completely naïve—after all, they had already met with deception and ill treatment from these officials. A guard was left at the courthouse in case of treachery. The identities of the guards and their numbers are a little hazy. They included those ultimately wounded, the between eight and twenty later captured and escapees such as Philip Safford. There is no record of Azariah Wright being present after Chandler left; he probably went home to act as host to a large number of out-of-town guests.

Meanwhile, Sheriff Paterson had retired to Norton's tavern, two doors down from Wright's, about a mile north of the courthouse, to "consult." He sent word to all Tories in the neighborhood to join him at once.

MRS. BRUSH AND MISS MONTUSAN

According to an account in the *Vermont Phoenix* of Brattleboro on Friday, March 22, 1805 (author unknown), the wife and stepdaughter of Crean Brush were in Westminster at the time and had words with the sheriff's party":

> *Mrs. Brush, who had been a widow Montusan, told them that if the judges were not women in men's clothes they would give the order to drive the rebels out of the courthouse at once, and bring the leaders to trial for treason; that they had authority and arms, and had only to contend with traitors who would run at the sound of their own voices. Her daughter, Frances Montusan, told her that she thought they had a just cause; and to remember that there were Green Mountain Boys on the other side of the mountains; and that Ethan Allen would come to assist them. Her mother answered that she should not be more surprised to see her sneaking after Ethan Allen than she was at that, and told the others that the girl was crazy, and Sheriff Paterson that the King expected him to do his duty…Frances Montusan became a widow Buchanan and was afterwards married, on February 16, 1784, to Ethan Allen at Westminster, and lived to great age in Burlington. This account of the part taken by her mother and herself was received from her many years after the occurrence.*

Did this ever happen? There is no reference to it in any contemporary account of the Massacre. It seems likely that Mrs. Brush and Fanny were in New York, where Crean Brush was serving in the General Assembly.

"Fire! God Damn You, Fire!"

A little before midnight, Paterson's men began to leave the tavern in small groups. They moved stealthily uphill toward the courthouse. It was a cold, moonlit night, but the men were well warmed with "fore gallons of rum" from Norton's tavern. According to the Whigs:

> *About midnight or a little before, the sentry at the door espyed some men with guns, and he gave the word to man the doors, and the walk was crowded. Immediately, the sheriff and his company marched up fast, within about ten rods of the door, and then the word was given, "take aim" and then "fire!" Three fired immediately. The word "fire" was repeated; "God damn you, fire! send them to hell!" was most or all the words that were to be heard for some time.*[52]

According to the Yorkers, Sheriff Paterson demanded in the king's name to be let in. He was not. He would come in quietly, he said, or he'd come in by force, and at the head of his men he climbed the three stairs. At the top the Whig guards pushed him back. He tried again, and this time he was clubbed to the ground by some unknown person. (A byword in southern Vermont for generations, born of this moment, was the mocking question, "Who hit Billy Paterson?" It may have alluded to another traditional part of the story: that Paterson was so drunk he fell down the stairs unaided.)

Whether he was felled by a blow or drunkenness or stayed on his own two feet, Billy Paterson was now a well-oiled and angry man. He ordered his men to fire. Three guns went off, the balls passing over the heads of the Whigs and lodging in the ceiling. According to the Yorkers, the next shots were fired from inside the courthouse, slightly wounding several of the posse and justifying all that happened next—a second, deadly volley from the posse, which then rushed the courthouse. The Whigs insisted that they were unarmed, and no shots came from within.

> *There were several men wounded; one was shot with four bullets, one of which went through his brain, of which wound he died the next day. Then they rushed in with their guns, swords and clubs, and did most cruelly*

One of the front doors to the courthouse, showing bullet damage from the Massacre. *Westminster Historical Society.*

mammock several more; and took some that were not wounded, and those that were, and crowded them all into close prison together, and told them that they should all be in hell before the next night, and that they did wish that there were forty more in the same case with that dying man. When they put him into prison, they took and dragged him as one would a dog; and would mock him as he lay gasping, and make sport for themselves at his dying motions.[53]

The dying man was William French, a twenty-one-year-old farmer from the Brattleboro/Dummerston border. His father, John French, had been a delegate to the third convention at Westminster only a month before. French's family lived at Fort Dummer for a time. Theophilus Crawford recalled

"Red Westminster"

Right: A bullet hole from a board above the courthouse door. Crean Brush transformed the initial scattering of shots in the first moments of the massacre to a careful, humanitarian warning volley. *Westminster Historical Society.*

Below: This saddlebag and other items of horse equipment are said to have belonged to William French. *Loaned by J.W. Collins to Westminster Institute; Westminster Historical Society.*

arriving at the fort in a dugout canoe during a driving May rainstorm as his family migrated to Westminster in 1768. When the Frenches realized they had company, William, then fourteen, ran down to the boat and carried five-year-old Theophilus up to the fort in his arms.

Now William lay bleeding on the cell floor. Two bullets had pierced his calf and thigh. Another struck him in the mouth, breaking out several teeth. The fourth entered his forehead, and a fifth lodged in his brain, just behind the ear. He struggled for breath but never regained consciousness. Hall says, "So closely was the prison crowded, that those who would have gladly bound up his wounds and spoken peace and consolation to the soul that still lingered in that bleeding and mangled body, were unable to act their wishes." Some three or four hours later Dr. William Hill of Westminster was allowed to visit French, but by then he was already dead.

Also wounded were Daniel Houghton of Dummerston, shot through the body; Jonathan Knight of Dummerston, with buckshot in his right shoulder; and a man named White of Rockingham, badly wounded in the knee. A fourth man from Dummerston had been hit on the head with a club and appeared to be dead.[54]

Accounts differ as to the number of prisoners taken. Depositions taken in New York later in March say eight or nine. According to the report of a Select Committee of the Vermont House in 1852, there were twenty prisoners. Hall says there were seven prisoners and ten wounded men. However many, they were too closely crowded even to tend the wounded. They could only listen to French die while the court party drank raucously in the room above.

Chapter 4
Government Overthrown

"Hatless to Dummerston"

Many of the defenders escaped through the side doors. Philip Safford, leader of the Rockingham men (and Azariah Wright's brother-in-law), fought his way out the front, shouting, "Don't run, boys, don't run, we'll go out the same way as we came in!" He knocked down eight or ten of the sheriff's men with his club and received several severe saber cuts on the head from Sheriff Paterson.

Safford and the other escapees must have arrived at their friends' houses within minutes of the sound of gunshots. The bad news was soon absorbed. The Whigs had been determined to avoid violence; now it had come to them. But firebrand Azariah Wright didn't gather his remnant of men to storm the courthouse. Instead, he sent word everywhere—the West Parish, Walpole, Rockingham. Reuben Jones rode "hatless" to Dummerston. Others went to Massachusetts and over the mountains to rouse the Green Mountain Boys. The result has been likened to a rising of the Highland clans of Scotland. "The people that escaped took prudent care to notify the people in the county, and also in the government of New Hampshire and the Bay; which being justly alarmed at such an unheard of and aggravated piece of murder, did kindly interpose in our favor."[55] By noon of the fourteenth there were four hundred armed men in Westminster, quadrupling the fighting-age male population. Benjamin Bellows brought his Walpole militia. Captain Stephen Sergent led a company from Rockingham. Guilford brought its organized militia, and the Westminster militia under Azariah Wright was out in full force.

Drum that belonged to Azariah Wright's militia. The exterior is red; the bands are blue, with yellow decorations. *Westminster Institute; loaned to Westminster Historical Society.*

On Tuesday, the 14ᵗʰ inst., about twelve o'clock, nearly 200 men, well armed, came from New Hampshire government; and before night there were several of the people of Cumberland county returned and took up all that they knew of, that were in the horrid massacre, and confined them under a strong guard; and afterwards they confined as many as they could get evidence against, except several that did escape for their lives.[56]

MEANWHILE, INSIDE THE COURTHOUSE...

In the jail, one prisoner lay dead, and several others were badly wounded. Upstairs, the court party was sobering, physically and mentally. They declared court open the next morning but took no regular action, instead writing up an account of the events of the night before. This version is closest in time to the event, written twelve hours later by (probably hungover) members of the court party. They worried that events "may Be represented very Different from what The same really was" and tried to get a jump on the news cycle of the day. The first newspaper publication of the event would be in the *Essex Gazette* of March 14–21. (For ease of reading I have broken this into paragraphs.)

New York County of Cumberland court of common Pleas, And court of General Sessions of the Peace holden at the court House in Westminster this Fourteenth Day of March A.D. 1775. Whereas a very melancholly and unhappy affair Happened at this Place in the evening of yesterday The thirteenth Instant and Whereas it may be that the Same may Be represented very Different From what The same really was We his majesty's Judges and Justices of the said Courts being chiefly there Present have Thought it our Duty thus to relate a true state of the Facts Exactly as they happened.

Many threats having for several Terms past been Thrown out by evil minded persons that they would With Violence break up and Destroy the courts of our Sovereign Lord the king in this county and threats of A more Daring and absolute nature than formerly having been thrown out by certain Evil Minded persons Against the setting of this present Court the Sheriff tho't it Essentially necessary to raise a Posse For the Courts Protection and having Raised about sixty Men armed some With Guns and some with staves he arrived At there head before the Court House about five o'clock In the afternoon of yesterday When to the Great Surprise of the said Sheriff and Posse they found the court house Taken into Possession and the several Doors thereof Guarded by a large number of Rioters (supposed to be about an Hundred in the whole) armed With clubs and some Few fire arms.

The Sheriff then endeavored to Go in at the Door of the court-house, but was prevented by Threats And menaces; whereupon he read the King's Proclamation, with a very loud voice commanding In his Majesty's name all persons unlawfully assembled Immediately to Depart, and thereupon Demanded Entrance again But was again refused and Prevented by threats and Menaces as Before.

The Sheriff then told the Rioters that he would Leave them a short time to consider of their behaviour And to Disperse, and if they would not afterwards allow Him Entrance into the said court-house That he would Absolutely Enter it by force. But the Rioters made scoff at this Measure replying the hardest must fend off.

*The Rioters a little time afterward wanted to choose committees to
Parley, but was answered that they could not Parley to consider whether the
King's Court Should proceed or not.*

*Judge Chandler informed them that if they had any real grievances
to complain of if they would Present a Petition to the court when sitting
it should be heard the Sheriff then gave the Posse Liberty To Refresh
themselves and about two Houers afterward He Brought the said Posse
Before the courthouse again and then again Demanded Entrance in his
majesty's Name but was again refused in like manner as Before.*

*Whereupon he told them that he would Absolutely enter it Either Quietly
or by force and commanded the Posse to follow close to him which they
Accordingly Did and getting near The Door he was struck several Blows
with clubs, which he had the Goodness in General to fend off so far at
least as not to Receive Any very Great Damage but several of their clubs
striking Him as he was goeing up the steps, and The Rioters Persisting in
maintaining Their Ground, he ordered some of the Posse to fire, which they
accordingly did.*

*The Rioters then fought Violently with their clubs, and fired some few
fire arms at the Posse by which Mr. Justice Butterfield received a slight shot
in the arm and another of the Posse received a slight shot in the head with
Pistol Bullets: but happily none of the Posse were mortally wounded.*

*Two persons of the Rioters were Dangerously wounded (one of whom
is since dead) and several others of the Rioters were also wounded, but not
Dangerously so. Eight of the Rioters were taken prisoners (including The
one which is since Dead) & the wounded were taken care of by Doct. Day,
Doct. Hill and Doct. Chase. The latter of which was immediately sent
for on Purpose.*

*The rest of the Rioters Dispersed giving out Threats that they would
collect all the force Possible and would return as on this Day to revenge
themselves on the Sheriff and on several others of the Posse.*

*This Being a true state of the facts without the least Exaggeration on the
one side or Diminution on the other We humbly submit to Every Reasonable
Inhabitant whether his majesty's courts of Justice the Grand and only
security For the life liberty and property of the publick should Be trampled
on and Destroyed whereby said persons and properties of individuals must
at all times be exposed to the Rage of a Riotous and Tumultuous assembly
or whether it Does not Behove Every of his Majesty's Liege subjects In the
said county to assemble themselves forthwith for the Protection of the Laws
and maintenance of Justice.*

Dated in open Court the Day and Year Aforesaid.

Thomas Chandler,
Noah Sabin,
Step'h Greenleaf,
Benj'a Butterfield,
Bildad Andross,
S. Gale, Clk.[57]

Noteworthy discrepancies in this "true state of the facts Exactly as they Happened" are the following:

No mention is made of refreshments at the Tory Tavern. The court account implies a much more reasonable hour than midnight for the final events of the day.

The Whigs, to their own mind peacefully assembled within, are described as "Rioters" and as "Tumultuous"—an interesting echo of the resolution of the first Westminster convention.

The Whigs are described as armed with firearms, a charge they always denied. According to Calvin Webb, eighteen years old and a Westminster resident at the time, though not present at the Massacre, "The liberty men had no guns when they first came, but after French was killed, they went home and got them." Theophilus Crawford said, "The Whigs had not so much as a pistol among them." Azariah Wright's grandson wrote to the historian Benjamin Hall, by the dictation of his father Salmon Wright, a boy of twelve or thirteen at the time of the Massacre: "There were no arms carried by the liberty party, except clubs which were obtained by the Rockingham Company at my grandfather's wood-pile. There were no Tories wounded, save those knocked down by the club of Philip Safford."[58]

Assertion isn't proof, but it's difficult to see why an armed party would take the last-minute decision to pick up clubs from a woodpile. If the Whigs had been armed, it seems likely that they would have used their guns effectively. Several were experienced soldiers. Of course, there may have been one or two pistols among the Whigs, even if the policy was officially against it; however, one would then expect some Whig or other to boast of it. But the Whig position was always that the slight wounds (if any) among the sheriff's party were the result of friendly fire. No account from the Whig side, either at the time or in later generations, mentions firearms among those inside the courthouse. The assertion that some had guns comes entirely from the Yorkers, who had strong reason to establish that they hadn't fired on an unarmed crowd.

This account also makes no mention of warning shots. The sheriff merely orders his men to fire. According to the Whigs, firing was scattered at first, and the sheriff bellowed at his men to keep firing. By the time the story reached the governor's council and the New York General Assembly, the initial three shots would be transformed into a careful, humanitarian warning volley. This seems out of keeping with the character of the event: drunken men in the dark and a furious sheriff who may have just been knocked downstairs.

No mention is made of the brutal treatment of the dying French. Instead, it is emphasized that Dr. Chase was "immediately sent for on Purpose."

The only Westminster resident to sign this statement, written within the courthouse among broken benches and bloodstained floors, was Bildad Andros.

TABLES TURNED

Having finished their account, the posse began to hear rumors:

> *In the afternoon they were suprized by an Account that a large party of armed men were coming over from New Hampshire & apprehending it might be with a Design to interrupt the Business the Court thought fit to adjourn to the ensuing June Term. That the Judges Sherif Clerk & officers remained at the Court House where they usually diet during the Sitting of the Court. That a few hours afterwards another party armed came in from Fulham and putney in the said County consisting of about forty, who as this Deponent then understood and verily believes, after putting it to a vote, declared that they would immediately fire into the Court House & kill & destroy every person there. That the Leaders of the party from New Hampshire interposed and prevented the horrid Resolution from being executed, by guarding all the Doors and passages into the Court House That the said Rioters from Fulham and Putney expressed the greatest Indignation and Concern in being disappointed of their intended Revenge & that many of them cried aloud with Vexation. That they next insisted that the Judges Sheriff Clerk & others who were thus in prison in the Court house should be closely confined in the Goal, to which the party from New Hampshire consented, and accordingly put them all in one of the prison Rooms; the Key of which was kept by one Butterfield the Head of the said New Hampshire party and there they were kept in close Custody from Wednesday Night until Sunday Noon.*[59]

When "the mob" returned, "two of them came into the Court House to the said Sheriff one of whom threatned and insulted the Sheriff and declared that the Judges should be brought out before the Mob and make acknowledgements to their satisfaction. That they would pull down the Court House. That the Sheriff and all that had a hand in perpetrating the horrid Massacre as he expressed himself should be taken into custody and put in irons."[60]

Hall describes the scene in the courthouse: "The benches were broken, and the braces, timbers, and studs of the unfinished room, were cut and battered by the bullets fired by the Tories, after they had obtained entrance into the building. Blood was to be seen in the passages, and the stairs were stained with stiffened gore."[61]

Townspeople were allowed inside in groups of four or five at a time to see the prisoners and French's body. Calvin Webb, eighteen-year-old son of Westminster's first schoolteacher, said:

> At the time of the Court-house affray, I lived in Westminster, but was not present at the scene. Heard of it the next day from a little man, familiarly known as Hussian Walker, a mighty flax-dresser, who was in the engagement. Soon after this I started off in company with several other youngsters, whose names I have forgotten. Many people were going in the same direction. It was about the middle of the day when I reached the Court-house, and soon after my arrival, I saw the body of French, who had been shot the night before. A sentry was stationed to guard the corpse, as it lay on the jail-room floor. The clothes were still upon it, as in life. The wounds seemed to be mostly about the head; the mouth was bloody, and the lips were swollen and blubbered.[62]

Joseph Hancock of the court party slipped out of the courthouse. There, as he later testified, he heard talk of firing on every person in the courthouse—this being prevented by the New Hampshire party.

Once the courthouse was secure and the sheriff and those inside confined,

> they sent out parties to pick up such of the Sheriff's party as they could find and to waylay the Roads that they should not escape...a Body of about twelve with a Leader [came] to Tavern in Westminster to apprehend one Knights an Attorney one Serjeant a Constable and the said William Williams all of the Sheriffs Posse. [T]he next morning about eight or nine o'clock the Deponent going towards the Court House saw a Party of the Rioters who had made Prisoner of Oliver Wells who is one of the son's of

Judge Wells and Mr Hill an Inhabitant of Westminster both of whom
they carried to and imprisoned in the Court House.

Apparently, Knight was not apprehended. He isn't on the list of prisoners, and according to a footnote in *The Rangers; or the Tory's Dauhter*, a novel written about the Massacre in 1851, Knight made his escape this way:

I have heard Judge Samuel Knight describe the trepidation that seized a
portion of the community, when, after the massacre, and on the rising of the
surrounding country, they came to learn the excited state of the populace.
He related how he and another member of the bar (Stearns, I think, who
was afterwards attorney-general of Nova Scotia) hurried down to the river,
and finding there a boat…they paddled themselves across and lay all day
under a log in the pine forest opposite the town; and when night came, went
to Parson Fessenden's at Walpole, and obtained a horse, so that, by riding
and tying, they got out of the country till the storm blew over.

This account disagrees with that in *Vermont: A Study of Independence* by Rowland Robinson, who states that the Connecticut was icebound.

Apparently Hancock had not been identified at this time as a member of the sheriff's posse, nor had Oliver Church, as both were free and walking openly on the street. That soon changed.

Shortly after this Leonard Spalding above mentioned charged the Deponent
with having been one of those who came to reinforce the Sheriff whereupon
he was surrounded stopt and examined but was at length permitted to go at
large upon proof being given that he was not an Inhabitant of this province.[63]

But Hancock was indeed one of the reinforcements, having been asked to go to Westminster by Oliver Church. He had come up from Brattleboro early on Tuesday morning.

Shortly after the Deponent saw Thomas Ellis one of the Sheriffs posse
seized by another Party of the Rioters and confined in the Court house
and soon after being at the House of Crean Brush Esquire he saw a fresh
party of about three hundred Rioters armed headed by Solomon Hervey of
Fulham Pratitioner of Physic who arrived with a Drum beating having
in their Custody four more of the Sheriffs party who being on their way
home had been intercepted…after they had been examined by them before

the Court House were dismissed first being disarmed and had a pass given them Signed by the said Solomon Hervey who was lately appointed a Colonel among them at a County Convention held about three weeks before at Westminster for Redress of Grievances when they appointed as the Deponent has heard and believes a variety of Field Officers to command their Forces.[64]

By now the Whigs had imprisoned most of the members of their former county government. The question was, what to do with them?

As the Deponent passed and repassed among the mob he observed that they were very violent and from what the Deponent heard them say to one another he is apprehensive of the worst consequences to the persons confined by them... some of the Mob speaking as tho' they were desirous to fire vollies thro the House others as tho' they wanted to have the Sheriff turned out to them and one man in particular said his flesh crawled to be tomahawking them.[65]

Help from Afar

All reports of threats from the crowd come from men in the pay of the court party. Despite the alleged violent words (again, we are told of these only by Yorker sources), no violent deeds were done other than imprisoning members of the posse. Still, the prisoners and their allies had good reason to be fearful. The established social and judicial order had been overturned. A popular young man lay on the courthouse floor, not yet twenty-four hours dead, and the crowd was angry.

They called those who are for supporting order and Government Tories and the Deponent heard many of the Rioters say they saw now what the damned Tories would be at that they were a pack of murderers and they wanted to serve them in their own kind.

When Samuel Gale's wife was allowed into the courthouse, he was able to whisper in her ear, asking that she send Hancock to her mother, Mrs. Wells, to get word to Colonel Wells and Crean Brush in New York "and send them relief without Delay at the same time desiring that she would send some Person upon whom no suspicion could fall for that he feared if the Rioters discovered the attempt they would massacre the Prisoners without mercy."[66]

An exaggerated fear? Though the deposition was apparently juiced up to create maximum urgency in the New York General Assembly, nonetheless these formerly powerful men were now helpless, imprisoned and surrounded by hundreds of their enemies, who had been greatly provoked. Gale's fear was no doubt perfectly genuine, and his wife must have shared it.

GREEN MOUNTAIN BOYS

The thrills of the day weren't over for Joseph Hancock. Mrs. Gale was able to drop a word in his ear, and he set off for Brattleboro with the men who had gotten the pass from Solomon Hervey.

> *They had not got a mile on their Journey before they were taken Prisoners again by another party of the Mob but were released upon producing the said pass…upon the road the Deponent saw Robert Cockran armed with a Sword and Pistols who said he was Captain of the Boys of the Green mountains That there was Fifty pounds reward offered for taking him and tauntingly asked why the Deponent and those that were with him did not attempt it… Cockran said he was going to Westminster to see the matter settled and have Revenge that he had left his Party passing the West River that he had heard that Lawyer Knights Josiah Arms of Brattleborough and Lieutenant Osgood of New Fane had assisted the Sheriff and that he would have them if they continued upon Earth that he would see who was for the Lord and who was for Balaam that shortly the Deponent met the party of the said Robert Cockran consisting of about forty or fifty men mostly armed.*[67]

Not all the Yorkers were imprisoned. Luke Knowlton of Newfane headed home on the fourteenth with eleven others.

> *Passing along a cross-road leading from Westminster to New Fane, the party stopped at the house of James Crawford and asked for something to drink. Mrs. Crawford, whose sentiments were the same as her husband's, replied, "we have no drink for murderers," and refused compliance with the request. Knowlton, who was a polite man, bowed as this answer was given, and went his way, as did his companions theirs, thirsting*[68]

The sheriff and an increasing number of the court party were confined, first in the courtroom itself. Later they were put into the cells. Accounts stress the crowded conditions the night of the Massacre, when the Whigs were imprisoned there. It must have been at least as crowded for the Tories; a large number were crammed in together for a much longer time, with their enemies coming in to look at them and make comments. They could doubtless hear any threats being made outside. We have no idea what the sanitary arrangements were, but it was certainly an unpleasant week for Sheriff Paterson and his friends.

The Whigs had overturned the county government, but they were not anarchists. On the fifteenth they set up a committee and held an inquest into French's death, under Timothy Olcott, the county coroner. French had been laid out by James Crawford, father of the little boy he once carried into Fort Dummer. His body lay in the courthouse, with many townspeople coming in to see it—some, we are told, to press their handkerchiefs into his blood.

> On the 15th inst., the body formed, chose a moderator and clerk, and chose a committee to see that the coroner's jury of inquest were just, impartial men; which jury on their oath did bring in that W. Patterson, etc., etc., did on the 13th March inst., by force and arms, make an assault on the body of William French, then and there lying dead, and shot him through the head with a bullet, of which wound he died and not otherwise.

> Report of the Coroner's Jury
> New York
> Cumberland County   An Inquisition Indented and
> Taken at Westminster the fifteenth Day of March one Thousand Seven
> Hundred and Seventy Five before me Tim° Olcott Gent one of the Corroners
> of the County afore Said upon the View of the Body of William French
> then and there Lying Dead upon the oaths of Thos Amsden John Avorll
> Joseph Pierce Nathanael Robertson Edward Hoton Michael Law George
> Earll Daniel Jewet Zachariah Gilson Ezra Robenson Nathaniel Davis
> Nathaniel DoubleDee John Wise Silas Burk Elihue Newel Alexr Pammerly
> Joseph Fuller Good and Lawfull men of the County afore Said who being
> Sworn to Enquire on the part of ouor Said Lord the King when where how
> and after what manner the Said Wm French Came to his Death Do Say
> upon their oaths that on the thirteenth Day of March Instant William
> Paterson Esqr Mark Langdon Cristopher Osgood Benjamin Gorton Samuel
> Night and others unknown to them assisting with force and arms made
> an assault on the Body of the Said Wm French and Shot him Through
> the Head with a Bullet of which wound he Died and Not Otherways in

*witness where of the Coroner as well as the Juryors have to this Inquision
put their hands and Seals att the place afore Said.*

Westminster jurors sitting on this inquest included John Averill, Nathanael
Robertson (Robinson), Ezra Robenson (Robinson), Nathanial Doubledee
(Doubleday) and Zachariah Gilson.

Those blamed for killing French include Paterson, Mark Langdon,
Cristopher Osgood, Benjamin Gorton, Samuel Night and "others unknown."
Though William and Billy Willard and Benjamin Baker were later said to
have been the killers, their names don't appear on this list. No one could
have known who fired the fatal shot. The action took place in dark, crowded
conditions. The attackers were the worse for rum; and we must remember
that firing squads have been used by the military, among other reasons, to
eliminate any certainty as to who had fired the fatal shot in an execution.

Hall asserts that William Willard, while still imprisoned in the courthouse,

The William French monument, showing the text
that appeared on French's original gravestone.
Michael Fawcett.

"made a brag that he
struck French" and
knocked him down. (The
quote is in the original and
unattributed.) Hall further
says that Willard, "after his
enlargement…went to New
York, and on his return,
appeared in a new suit of
clothes, which, it was said,
had been given him by the
Lieutenant Governor, in
acknowledgement of his
valiant conduct."[69]

On the other hand,
William Czar Bradley
believed that it was Billy
Willard who had bragged
of killing French. Billy
Willard's daughter married
Bradley's father; Bradley
knew both Willards, first
as neighbors and then
as family members. And

Benjamin Baker is said to have hidden in a Halifax cellar for a week, fearing retribution as French's killer.[70] But whatever the Willards and Baker may have said later, they were known at the time only as members of the court party that stormed the courthouse. We are forced to conclude that William French was killed by persons unknown and leave it at that.

French was buried late on the fifteenth, after the inquest was complete. We don't know if his parents came to Westminster to say farewell. He was buried with military honors; the militias of surrounding towns fired a salute over his grave. As Hall imagined it:

> *The smoke rolled off from the freshly turned earth, and as the thunder of the musketry echoed over the beautiful plains of Westminster and reverberating among the distant hills, finally died away into silence; those determined men who had gathered at the sepulture of the first victim to American Liberty and the principles of freedom, vowed to avenge the wrongs of their oppressed country, and kindled in imagination the torch of war, which so soon after blazed like a beacon-light at Lexington and Bunker Hill.[71]*

Purple prose notwithstanding, the militiamen certainly had revenge on their minds, and the report of the committee reflects an awareness of American liberty and the wrongs done against it.

The wounded were cared for at Azariah Wright's house, except for Daniel Houghton. He lay in the home of Eleazer Harlow, very close to the courthouse, perhaps because his wound was too severe for him to be moved.

THE PRISONERS

After the inquest the sheriff's men were put into the cells. Next they were formally accused by a self-appointed ad hoc body.

> *Then the criminals were confined in close prison and, on the evening of the same day and early the next morning, a large number came from the southern part of the county of Cumberland, and the Bay Province. It is computed, that in the whole, there were 500 good martial soldiers, well equipped for war, that had gathered.*
>
> *On the 16th inst., the body assembled; but being so numerous that they could not do business, there was a vote passed, to choose a large committee to represent the whole, and that this committee should consist of men who*

did not belong to the county of Cumberland, as well as of those that did belong thereto; which was done. After the most critical and impartial examination of evidence, voted, that the heads of them should be confined in Northampton jail, till they could have a fair trial; and those that did not appear so guilty, should be under bonds, holden to answer at the next court of oyer and terminer in the county aforesaid; which was agreed to. On the 17th inst., bonds were taken for those that were to be bound, and the rest set out under a strong guard for Northampton.

We, the committee aforesaid, embrace this opportunity to return our most grateful acknowledgements and sincere thanks to our truly wise and patriotic friends in the government of New Hampshire and the Massachusetts Bay, for their kind and benevolent interposition in our favor, at such a time of distress and confusion aforesaid; strongly assuring them, that we shall be always ready for their aid and assistance, if by the dispensation of divine providence, we are called thereto.

Signed by order of the Committee.
Reuben Jones, Clerk.
Cumberland County, March 23d, 1775

Why Northampton? The Report of the Select Committee in 1858 (Vermont legislature) notes that Northampton "was then the head quarters of the disaffected in Western Massachusetts, with whom the Cumberland County Whigs had a friendly and familiar intercourse which continued for several years after."

Released under bond were Thomas Chandler, chief judge; Bildad Easton (Westminster), deputy sheriff; Captain Benjamin Burt (Westminster); Thomas Sergeant; Oliver Wells; Joseph Willard (Westminster, age fifteen); and John Morse (Westminster). They gave their bonds with security to John Hazeltine to appear and take their trial at the appointed time. No charge was brought against Thomas Ellis, and he was freed.

Sent to jail in Northampton were Noah Sabin, one of the side judges; Benjamin Butterfield, an assistant justice; William Willard (Westminster), justice of the peace; William Paterson (Westminster), high sheriff; Samuel Gale, clerk of the court; Benjamin Gorton, deputy sheriff; Richard Hill; William Williams; and one Cunningham.

With Crean Brush and Samuel Wells absent in New York, the power structure of Cumberland County was essentially decapitated by these imprisonments. The militias and their leaders were in charge, conducting business by democratic vote.

Jones's rather chaste account leaves out some dramatic details. One was the arrival of Robert Cockran with forty Green Mountain Boys, all wearing sprigs of hemlock in their caps. Cockran had been involved with Ethan Allen in actions west of the Green Mountains, and there was a reward of fifty pounds for his arrest. He added greatly to the noise and sense of menace in Westminster, according to John Griffin, a Brattleboro farmer who followed Church and Hancock to New York a few days later.

> *On the Wednesday Evening as he* [Griffin] *thinks Robert Cockran proposed to destroy the Court house and all the persons in it and declared that he would beat up for volunteers the next morning, that this he accordingly did the next Day & inlisted (as this Deponent was informed and verily believes) about one hundred Men that it was then put to vote by this Company (as this Deponent then understood & verily believes) whether they should burn the Court House and all who were in it and it was determined in favor of this inhuman Resolution; but that the party from New Hampshire again interposed and prevented its taking effect…Cockran and his party frequently proposed trying the said Magistrates and officers of Justice by a Court Martial and punishing them on the Spot; but this was prevented also by the New Hampshire party.*[72]

There is considerable discrepancy between these versions of events. The deponents describe the threats in lurid tones: the threat to burn the courthouse with everyone inside; the man whose "flesh crawled to be tomahawking them." The flesh of the listeners must have crawled on hearing it—if it was ever said. It must be remembered that these depositions were intended to jar the New York General Assembly into acting, which may explain the emphasis on blood-curdling threats.

Reuben Jones's narrative, on the other hand, is biased toward the cool and cerebral. It seems unlikely that things were actually that cool, considering the violence that had taken place and the rough character of some of the men who gathered: Green Mountain Boys, former Rangers and other veterans of the French and Indian War.

Whether viewed as "the Mob" or as "the good people," it was an enormous crowd gathered in this small frontier town. Where did they all sleep? Who fed them—and where did the food come from? Who fed the extra horses that poured into town? Most of the men likely walked, but a large number must have ridden. This was March; hay, corn and other winter-stored provisions would be running short even without five hundred extra mouths to feed. It was cold for sleeping outdoors or in barns—but where else could the men have slept? There were at most twenty-five houses, most of them smallish log cabins, in the village of Westminster. Did the militias come prepared to bivouac outdoors? We can imagine a military encampment in the fields around the courthouse, with small fires burning and men gathered around them. We can imagine (with a high degree of probability) that the taverns were crowded and a brisk business done there. We can imagine women with a lot of extra cooking to do and not many supplies to do so with and children running around in a high state of excitement. Unfortunately, all we can do is imagine. No contemporary description of the scene has come down to us.

"ANARCHY AND CONFUSION"

Church and Hancock reached New York on March 20, having traveled for 110 hours. (The trip today takes approximately 4 hours.) On hearing what they had to say, Brush and Wells informed Lieutenant Governor Colden, who called his council together the next day and informed them that "violent Outrages and Disorders" had happened in Cumberland County.

The council was then briefed. We don't know who did the talking; Wells, Brush, Church and Hancock all appeared together. The council reported as follows:

> *Report of the Governor's Council*
> *In Council March 21ˢᵗ 1775*
>   *His Honor the Lieutenant Governor informed the Council, that he had called them together in Consequence of his having received Information of some Violent Outrages and Disorders which have lately happened on the County of Cumberland, that he had requested Coll Wells and Crean Brush Esqr the Representatives of the said County to attend with the Persons who are said to have brought the Intelligence...Mr Brush informed his Honor and the Board that on Monday the 13ᵗʰ day of this Inst. about eighty Persons assembled and took Possession of the Court House in Westminster in the County of Cumberland, in order to prevent the opening and holding of the Courts...That they were in Part Armed and it was then said that others were gathering and arming to join them. That the Sherif and Magistrates Assembled and sent several Messages to the Rioters desiring and warning them to leave the Court*

House, that they repeatedly refused and violently drove from the Door the said Messengers. That the Sherif and Magistrates then went to the Court House and by Public Proclamation required the Mob to depart, and upon their refusal the Magistrates ordered three Guns to be fired into the Room, but above the Door and in such a manner as not to injure their Persons, That thereupon the Mob returned the Fire upon the Magistrates and their Assistants and wounded Mr Justice Butterfield, when the Magistrates fired upon the said Mob and a Violent affray ensued, in which one of the Rioters was killed and nine wounded, That on the next day the Justices opened the said Court and were proceeding to Business when a number of Persons partly of the said County and partly from the Provinces of the Massachusetts Bay and New Hampshire assembled, Surrounded the Court House and made the Judges Sheriff Clerk of the said Court and several other Persons their Prisoners, and have Confined them in the County Gaol, that one Cockran who is a notorious Ringleader of the Riots at Bennington, was a principal in the Mob, and that the Rioters have threatned to try by their own Authority the Magistrates and others whom they have taken Prisoners for the Massacry, as they Term it, which they have committed—And the said Coll Wells, Mr Brush and the Expresses being withdrawn: His Honor required the advice of the Council in this Emergency.

The Council humbly advise that the two Persons who came Express do severally put into Writing the particular Circumstances relating to the Affair and attest to the same, and that his Honor do send the said Depositions to the General Assembly together with a Message warmly urging them to proceed immediately to the consideration of this important Intelligence and adopt some effectual Measures by which a total stop may be put to Evils of so Alarming a Nature, and the principal Aiders and Abettors of such Violent Outrages brought to Condign Punishment.

Warning Shots Invented

Church and Hancock left Westminster on March 14; by their evidence the word "massacre" was already being used to describe the events at the courthouse, where armed members of New York government fired on peaceful protestors.

Somewhere on the long road between Westminster and council chambers in New York, Paterson's ragged volley of shots was transformed. Whether that reflected Church and Hancock's own thinking or the editing of Wells and Brush or if events were reinterpreted by Colden and his council is impossible to say. Compare the following three statements:

- *He ordered some of the Posse to fire, which they accordingly did. (March 14, court statement)*
- *And then the word was given, "take aim" and then "fire!" Three fired immediately. The word "fire" was repeated; "God damn you, fire! send them to hell!" (March 23, Ruben Jones's report)*
- *The Magistrates ordered three Guns to be fired into the Room, but above the Door and in such a manner as not to injure their Persons." (report of Governor's Council, after hearing from Church, Hancock, Wells and Brush)*

Two out of three versions—including one supplied by the court party—indicate that Paterson gave no order for a warning volley. He simply ordered his men to fire; three did ineffectually, and with profane encouragement from their leader, and the rest of the posse did a little better. The prim phrase "in such a manner as not to injure their Persons" seems a lawyerly after-the-fact invention that Hancock and Church repeated in their deposition.

Hall casts doubt on the veracity of these depositions. "The depositions, although given under oath, had been previously supervised by the Tory representatives in the Legislature of New York from Cumberland county, and were, no doubt, colored by them in such a manner as to make the cause of the Whigs appear in its worst light. Men, most violent in the measures which they were ready to adopt to suppress the first outbreathings of liberty and right, were not those who would scruple to exaggerate and falsify in order to achieve the ends they had proposed."[73] Hall offers no direct evidence of coaching, but the story certainly evolved to the credit of the court party.

DEPOSITIONS

The council advised the two messengers—called "expresses"—to put their information in the form of a deposition, which they did the next day. A later express, John Griffin, was deposed on the twenty-seventh or twenty-eight. Church said of the men in the courthouse:

Many...had Fire Arms and the rest in general had Staves [and] they appeared very riotous and Tumultuous...

*Several of the said Rioters and in Particular one Charles Davenport of
Fulham in the said County of Cumberland Carpenter cried out that that
they would stay as long as they pleased and that neither the said Sheriff
or any of his men should have entrance there and that if he offered to take
possession of the said Court House they would send him and all his men
to Hell in fifteen minutes.*

Church was not an eyewitness to the Massacre but named Leonard
Spaulding of Putney and Hosea Miller and Daniel Sergeant of Fulham
as being "principally active" among the Whigs. He also named Fairbank
Moore Jr. and Elias Wilder Junior of Fulham (Dummerston).

Hancock, arriving on the scene the next day, reported chiefly about the
aftermath, especially the threats of violence. He is the source for the "flesh
crawled to be tomohawking them" line and Cockran's Balaam quote, and
he puts forward a theory that if the Whigs knew help was being sent for, they
would "massacre the Prisoners without mercy."

John Griffin arrived in New York a week later. He may have been a witness
to the Massacre, though that isn't clear. He says, "It is said and generally
understood that the first fire from the Sheriffs posse was only intended to
intimidate the Rioters the Guns having been directed to be and accordingly
were raised with that Intent so high as that charges might pass over the
Heads of the Rioters." Since the only order Paterson is known to have given
was "Fire!" this would have to have been a preset plan.

Griffin states:

*The principale and most active among the Rioters who took possession
of the Court house manner aforesaid were Doctor Jones of Rockingham,
Leonard Spalding of Putney, Charles Davenport, one Haven a Blacksmith,
Daniel Sergeant one Hooker, one Knight, Hosea Miller, Paul Gates and
Thomas Boyden all of Fulham. That the principal and most active of the
Rioters who were concerned in the other of the said Rioutous proceedings
were, besides the said Robert Cockran, Soloman Harvey of Fulham, Alijah
(Abijah) Lovejoy of Westminster & Othniel Wilkins of Guildford...That
two prisoners who were confined for Debt in the said Goal were discharged.
And the Deponent further saith, that he understood that the said Goal was
nailed up by Order of the Rioters and left empty in that Condition.*

Rumors of violent threats circulated immediately. A story published in the
New York Journal on March 23 was likely influenced by the stories of Church,

Hancock and Griffin. It concludes:

> *The mob, stimulated by their leaders to the utmost fury and revenge, breathed nothing but blood and slaughter against the unfortunate persons in their power. The only thing which suspended their fate was a difference of opinion as to the manner of destroying them. And from the violence and inhumanity of the disposition apparent in the rioters, it is greatly to be feared that some of the worthy men in confinement will fall a sacrifice to the brutal fury of a band of ruffians, before timely aid can be brought to their assistance.*

An afterthought to Church and Hancock's deposition, in the form of a short paragraph, was sworn to on the same day. It, too, seems to bear the hallmarks of Crean Brush's coaching.

> *The pretext for the Discontents in the said County of Cumberland as given out by some is that many persons were sued for Debts and were at the same Time unable to recover what is due to them in the province of the Massachusetts Bay and that they believe a design was formed and entred upon for shutting up the Courts of Justice to prevent those who were in Debt from being prosecuted by their Creditors.*

Hedged by "given out by some" and "they believe," this statement intersects neatly with a paragraph in Cadwallader Colden's letter to Lord Dartmouth a week or so later.

HOUGHTON DIES

On the same day that Church and Hancock were deposed, Daniel Houghton died in the home of Eleazer Harlow on the brow of Courthouse Hill. Houghton never received his due as a martyr of the Massacre. At the time of the inquest, he was expected to live. He was buried in the Westminster cemetery, where Hall says "for many years there was a stone, shapeless and unhewn, which marked the spot where he lay; but even this slight memorial has at length disappeared from its place, and no one can now [1852] mark with accuracy the locality of his grave."

Daniel Houghton's grave site was never permanently marked, and its location is unknown. His only memorial is this, on one face of the French monument. *Michael Fawcett.*

"TRUE BENEVOLENCE, REAL FRUGALITY"

On March 23, Church and Hancock's deposition was sent to the General Assembly, accompanied by an elegantly written message from Cadwallader Colden arguing that it would be kinder and more economical to punish the miscreants now than to have to punish them more severely later:

> GENTLEMEN: *You will see, with just indignation, from the papers I have ordered to be laid before you, the dangerous state of anarchy and confusion which has lately arisen in Cumberland county, as well as the little respect which has been paid to the provisions of the Legislature, at their last sessions, for suppressing the disorders which have for some time greatly disturbed the north-eastern districts of the county of Albany and part of the county of Charlotte.*

You are called upon, gentlemen, by every motive of duty, prudence, policy, and humanity, to assist me in applying the remedy proper for a case so dangerous and alarming.

The negligence of government will ever produce a contempt of authority, and fostering a spirit of disobedience, compel, in the sequel, to greater severity. It will therefore be found to be not only true benevolence, but also real frugality, to resist these enormities at their commencement; and I am persuaded, from your known regard to the dignity of government, and your humanity to the distressed, that you will readily strengthen the hands of civil authority, and enable me to extend the succour and support which are necessary for the relief and protection of his Majesty's suffering and obedient subjects, the vindication of the hour, and the promotion of the peace and felicity of the colony.[74]

His polished sentences notwithstanding, Colden seems to have expected little from the politically divided General Assembly, and he wasn't disappointed. After a vote of fourteen to nine in favor of enabling "the inhabitants of the county of Cumberland to reinstate and maintain the due administration of justice in that county, and for the suppression of riots," the issue of money was raised.

Crean Brush moved "that the sum of one thousand pounds be granted to his majesty, to be applied for the purposes enumerated in the report." After a vigorous debate, the motion carried by twelve to ten. "Every Whig present and several of the ministerial party, voted against the measure, and in the majority of two the vote of the Speaker was included."[75]

"A DANGEROUS INSURRECTION"

In an April 5 letter to Lord Dartmouth in which he also reports about actions of the "Bennington Rioters," Lieutenant Governor Colden mentioned the disturbances in Cumberland County. In the second paragraph, he revealed his feelings toward the gentlemen of the General Assembly and issued a chill threat to beggar the participants in the Massacre.

I have lately received accounts likewise, my Lord of a dangerous Insurrection in Cumberland County of this Province which is connected with Massachusetts Bay on one side and New Hampshire on the other. A number of People in Cumberland, worked up by the example and Influence of Massachusetts Bay, embraced the dangerous resolution of shutting up the Courts of Justice.

With this design they took Possession of the Court House, immediately before the Courts of General Sessions of the Peace, and common Pleas, were to be opened there in March last. They persisted with so much obstinacy to resist the Sheriff and his Posse that he was obliged to have recourse to fire arms, by which one of the Rioters were killed and several were wounded upon which they quitted the House and the Courts were opened. But by the next day such numbers had joined the Rioters from New Hampshire and Massachusetts Bay, as made them too powerfull for the Magistrates. they took one of the Judges the Sheriffs clerk of the Court and several other persons prisoners and after confining them for several days in the Goal of their own County carried them into Massachusetts Bay, and put them into the Goal of North Hampton where they remained when the last accounts came from them.

It was necessary for me, my Lord, to call upon the Assembly for aid, to reinstate the authority of Government in that country and to bring the atrocious offenders to Punishment. They have given but one thousand Pounds for this Purpose which is much too small a sum, but the party in the Assembly who have opposed every measure that has a tendency to strengthen or support Government by working on the parcemonious disposition of some of the Country Members had too much influence on this occasion I am now waiting for an answer from General Gage to whom I Have wrote on this affair in Cumberland: by his Assistance I hope I shall soon be able to hold a Court of Oyer and Terminer in that County, where I am assured there are some hundreds of the inhabitants well affected to Government; and if the Debts of the people who have been concerned in this outrage, were all paid, there would not be a sixpence of property left among them.

It is proper your Lordship should be informed, that the inhabitants of Cumberland County have not been made uneasy by any dispute about the Title of their Lands; those who have not obtained Grants under this Governm(t) live in quiet possession under the Grants formerly made by New Hampshire. The Rioters have not pretended any such pretext for their conduct. the example of Massachusetts Bay is the only reason they assigned. Yet I make no doubt they will be joined by the Bennington Rioters, who will endeavor to make one common cause of it, though they have not connection but in their violence to Government.[76]

Colden had no doubt that he was dealing with "a dangerous insurrection." He firmly separated it from the ongoing troubles in Bennington. This wasn't about New York jurisdiction; it was a rebellion against His Majesty's courts, directly inspired by the Massachusetts Farmers' Revolution.

GENERAL GAGE RESPONDS

It was commonly reported at the time that General Gage sent arms to New York in response to Colden's letter. They were brought by a boat called the *King's Fisher*. Samuel Wells of Brattleboro, the chief judge of Cumberland County, was called to testify about this on September 12, 1775, before the Committee of Safety of the New York Provincial Congress. By now New York had joined the rest of the colonies in resisting Britain, and Wells was suspected of "having been engaged in an attempt to introduce arms into Cumberland county in behalf of Great Britain, for the purpose of reinstating and maintaining the administration of justice therein."[77]

Wells confirmed that the arms had been sent for and did arrive, but

> the affair at Lexington put an end to it—of the £1,000 granted for Cumberland county, 720 of the money has been received—it was employed to reimburse the sheriff and Mr. Gale, the expense of themselves and the other prisoners and expresses—heard the arms were put on board the King's Fisher—has forgot how he heard it, and does not know how they were disposed of.[78]

The revolutionary events at Westminster were overshadowed by Lexington and Concord. But what if that hadn't happened? Cadwallader Colden—benevolently, frugally—was determined to restore order. Had he sent troops, the Patriots of New Hampshire and Massachusetts Bay would hardly have stood by while their neighbors were shot or hanged. Had Lexington not intervened, the Revolutionary War might have started in Westminster, and "the shot heard 'round the world" might be the one that killed William French.

PRISONERS RELEASED

The prisoners were confined in Northampton for two weeks. On April 10, the *New York Gazette* declared that "the gentlemen who had fallen into the hands of the insurgents" would be brought under a writ of habeas corpus to New York, where they would be charged. We know they had reached New York by May 3, but by then the Massachusetts insurrection had turned into a full-blown revolution. Apparently the prisoners spent at least a month in New York, perhaps lacking the funds to return home. That was soon remedied.

CONVENTION

In Westminster, a county convention was held on April 1, less than a month after the Massacre. Blood still stained the floor of the courthouse, and bullets were embedded in the door and beams. The minutes speak for themselves:

> *At a meeting of Committees appointed by a large body of inhabitants on the east side of the range of Green Mountains, held at Westminster, on the 11th day of April, 1775.*
>
> *1. Voted, That Major Abijah Lovejoy be the Moderator of this meeting.*
>
> *2. Voted, that Dr. Reuben Jones be the Clerk.*
>
> *3. Voted, as our opinion, That our inhabitants are in great danger of having their property unjustly, cruelly, and unconstitutionally taken from them, by the arbitrary and designing administration of the government of New York; sundry instances having already taken place.*
>
> *4. Voted, as our opinion, that the lives of those inhabitants are in the utmost hazard and imminent danger, under the present administration, Witness the malicious and horrid massacre of the night of the 13th ult.*
>
> *5. Voted, as our opinion, That it is the duty of said inhabitants, as predicated on the eternal and immutable law of self-preservation, to wholly renounce and resist the administration of the government of New York, till such time as the lives and property of those inhabitants may be secured by it; or till such time as they can have opportunity to lay their grievances before his most gracious Majesty in Council, together with a proper remonstrance against the unjustifiable conduct of that government; with a humble petition, to be taken out of so oppressive a jurisdiction, and, either annexed to some other government, or erected and incorporated into a new one, as may appear best to the said inhabitants, to the royal wisdom and clemency, and to such time as his Majesty shall settle this controversy.*
>
> *6. Voted, That Colonel John Hazeltine, Charles Phelps, Esq., and Colonel Ethan Allen, be a Committee to prepare such remonstrance and petition for the purpose aforesaid.*[79]

Compared with the last document from the pen of Reuben Jones, this has a much more conciliatory tone toward "his gracious Majesty" and an angrier tone toward New York. This may have something to do with the presence in Westminster of the Bennington element. The presence of Ethan Allen on a Cumberland County committee is a bit of a surprise, but as Cadwallader

Colden had predicted, the Bennington crowd now sought to make common cause with the Cumberland County rioters. But events moved quickly in 1775. The status quo of April 11 held for exactly three days. Then came Lexington and Concord.

BUSINESS AS USUAL

Revolution might have broken out in Massachusetts, but business went on as usual in New York. In a May 4 letter to Cadwallader Colden, Wells, Paterson and Gale held out their hands for a share of the £1,000 appropriated to restore peace in Cumberland County. Wells asked to be repaid for defraying the expenses of Church, Hancock, Griffin and others, to the tune of £43, fourteen shillings and sixpence. He claimed that the messengers "seem to have been of very essential service, in disheartning several of the late Rioters; and your Petitioners are humbly of opinion (from the last accounts) That had it not been for the late unhappy differences in Massachusetts-Bay, the Rioters would have been so far disheartned, as that the well disposed inhabitants, would have been able to have restored Peace in that County."[80]

It's difficult to see how the dispatching of three or four messengers could have "disheartned" the Whigs, and there's no particular evidence that anyone in Cumberland County was even aware that they had been sent.

Paterson asked to be reimbursed for defraying the expenses of the posse. Essentially this was a bar bill, amounting to seventy-seven pounds, twelve shillings and eleven pence farthing. Gale put in for traveling expenses for the people imprisoned, thirty-two pounds, fifteen shillings and halfpence, over and above forty pounds he had already received, for their living expenses in New York (thirty-one pounds, six shillings and six pence half-penny, and for a further thirty shillings for each of them to enable them to get back home).

These monies were paid out. It's unknown what happened to the rest of the appropriation. William Willard supposedly came home with a new coat, his reward for killing French, but there's no documentary evidence of that.

Two years later, in 1777, several members of the court party (including William Willard and John Norton) were among twenty-seven "fellow sufferers" seeking compensation for the "expence, trouble and loss of time" they had incurred due to their loyalty to New York. In their petition to Governor Clinton and the New York Senate and Assembly, they "humbly conceive[d] themselves clearly Entitled to a Compensation for their Losses and sufferings which Compensation if agreeable to your Excelency and honours they would wish to receive by a Grant of vacant and unappropriated Lands within this State of New York." William Willard lists himself as one who was "Confined by the Mob and Ill Treated." John Norton merely says "Supported New York." The claims were denied.[81]

The Massacre Assessed

Until well into the twentieth century, it was axiomatic among Vermont historians that the Westminster Massacre was the first bloodshed and first battle of the American Revolution. By the year 2000, the claim that it was a Revolutionary event was disparaged, and the words "Westminster Massacre" were frequently enclosed in belittling quotation marks.

But looked at objectively, the event and particularly its aftermath seem clearly revolutionary. Cumberland County Whigs wished (and voted) to comply with an early act of the Continental Congress. The protesters at Westminster were attempting to dissociate themselves from the noncomplying province of New York. Later writers have conflated this conflict with the ongoing disturbances around Bennington, but on March 13, 1775, the Westminster Massacre had nothing to do with the New Hampshire/New York dispute. Cumberland County rebelled for two reasons: maladministration of the courts and New York's lack of compliance with the Articles of Association. They were rebelling against New York as a byproduct of rebellion against the Crown.

Nonviolent protest was met with lethal violence. In response, the whole county rose, with assistance from neighboring colonies. The government of Cumberland County was overturned in a day, and if the "expresses" are to be believed, only the firm opposition of a few strong-minded leaders prevented a bloodbath.

The Westminster Massacre was eclipsed within a month by Lexington and Concord. The arms sent by General Gage to suppress the insurrection in Cumberland County were never deployed. But people in and around Cumberland County experienced all this as a continuum. From the actions at Salem that backed down Gage's army, to the mass protests that stopped the Massachusetts courts, to the protest at the Westminster Courthouse, to Lexington and Concord—they were all revolutionary acts, with the first deaths indisputably at Westminster.

After the Massacre, the residents of Cumberland County were prepared to use arms to oppose a government that had killed two of its citizens. The world changed, even more thoroughly than in Worcester or Springfield. In Massachusetts, the courts were stopped and a few officials were forced to resign. In Vermont, an entire county government was overturned, and a new, ad hoc government was set up.

On the other hand, the immediate official reaction of the Fourth Westminster Convention was to seek independence from New York, not Great Britain. Without being on the scene, it's impossible to assess the mix of feelings—how much those were homegrown and how much influenced by the Bennington element. Political opinions were fast moving in that eventful year. The "arbitrary and designing" government of New York of April 11 became "our New York brethren" by June 9.

Many residents of Westminster had divided loyalties. Crean Brush remained true to New York and Britain. John Norton did too, in his heart of hearts, yet he held office in Westminster and the county. Benjamin Burt, arrested as a member of the court party after the Massacre, later became very active in the cause of American independence. The situation, and these men, must not be oversimplified.

It's common in modern times to chuckle at the term massacre as applied to Westminster, since only two people were killed. It's worth remembering that only four people were killed at Kent State, also called a massacre, and for the same reason: armed agents of the government fired on unarmed protestors. In 1775, the Whigs called it a massacre, the Yorkers a riot and Cadwallader Colden an insurrection.

William French's gravestone inscription reflects a revolutionary view of the Massacre; we don't know when it was composed, and it may postdate Lexington and Concord.

> *In Memory of* WILLIAM FRENCH
> *Son to Mr. Nathaniel French. Who*
> *Was Shot at Westminster March ye 13th,*
> *1775, by the hands of Cruel Ministerial tools*
> *Of George ye 3d, in the Courthouse at a 11*
> * a Clock*
> *at Night in the 22d year of his Age.*

> HERE WILLIAM FRENCH *his Body lies.*
> *For Murder his Blood for Vengeance cries*
> *King Georg the third his Tory crew*
> *tha with a Bawl his head Shot threw.*

Government Overthrown

For Liberty and his Countrys Good
he Lost his Life his Dearest blood.

The Massacre was mentioned in at least three songs: the one referring to "the Youth of Red Westminster" and two local songs, one Tory and one Whig. The Tory song was written by John Arms, son of a Westminster proprietor. He was fifteen in 1775 and later changed his opinions, as noted in a vote of the Council of Vermont passed June 15, 1782, which said Arms joined "the enemies of this and other American States, and afterwards returned and asked pardon, was forgiven and restored to privileges of the State" on taking the oath of allegiance.

March y[e] thirteenth, in Westminster, there was a dismal clamor,
A mob containing five hundred men, they came in a riotous manner,
Swearing the courts they should not set, not even to adjournment,
But for fear of the Sheriff and his valient men, they for their fire-arms sent.
The Protestants that stood by the law, they all came here well armed;
They demanded the house which was their own, of which they were
*   debarred.*
The Sheriff then drew off his men to consult upon the matter,
How he might best enter the hous and not to make a slaughter.
The Sheriff then drew up his men in order to make a battle,
And told them for to leave the house or they should feel his bullets rattle.
But they resisted with their clubs until the Sheriff fired,
Then with surprise and doleful cries they all with haste retired.
Our valient men entered the house, not in the least confounded,
And cleared the rooms of every one, except of those who were wounded.[82]

The Whig song seems a bit more singable:

Come all you gallent hearts of gold
You people all both young and old
Doleful tragedy I know
I shall relate with grief and woe

At Westminster, a town in York
Where libertines they there did work
With staff in hand we only went
To stop the court was our intent

This and next two pages: This poem on the Massacre is by an unknown author. The manuscript looks like someone's attempt to write it down from memory. *Westminster Historical Society.*

1 Come all you galant hearts of gold
you people all both young and old
~~A dolful ~~geda & no i shall
adoleful tragy'a i know
i shall relate with greeat and wo

2 At westminster a town in york
where libertines they their did meeth
with staff in hand we onely went
to stop the court was our intent

3 but we had not been their long
before the ~~torys~~ apried strong
with arms complete all in oor sight
for to begin a blody fight

4 they marched and wield a fife now
in order for to have oor life
if that the hause they could not take
but the doors we did keep

5 thay coursd and semed to be mad
they held a councel that was bad
the torys from the court house went
to seek oor wo was their intent

6 to knont oons where may drank their fill
in order our blood to spill
to raise their shirits and make them led
to fine down men with out controll

7 and now we leave them their a while
for to behold their cursed guilt
and now a judas doth apear
to betray us most severe

8 it is Colonoll Chandler whom i mene
kind sir i ment for to bee plain
for he now with us did agree
to stope the court for libeity

9 it is onely murder roberry and theft
and same thought it would bee best
for that part of the court to stand
wee did agree with heart and hand

10 att ten or twelue oclock att night
their than begon a blody fight
our men were croded att the door
forty or fifty if not more

11 all in an alley long and larg
where twenty gune war all discharg
upon the son of liberty
so they should not go free

12 but the greate god was our defence
their war none slain but william french
a prity youth near twenty one
he was his fathers loving son

13 but of the rest their are now fiue
that narely escapt their liues wih them liues
for their war wounded best or more
wih french bay blesing to gean

— 13 1776
Lines Composed on the masacree at westminster March
by an eye witness and was wounded

40

Government Overthrown

But we had not been there long
Before the tories appeared strong
With arms complete all in our sight
For to begin a bloody fight

They marched now and with a fife
In order for to have our life
If that the house they could not take
But the doors we did keep

They cersed and seemed to be mad
They held a coucil that was bad
The tories from the court house went
To seek our woe was their intent

To Norton where they drank their fill
In order our blood to spill
To rais their spirits and make them bold
To fire down men without control

And now we have them there awhile
For to behold their cursed guile
And now a judge doth appear
To betray us most severe

It is Colonel Chandler whom I mean
Kind sir, I mind for to be plain
For he now with us did agree
To stop the court for liberty

It is only murder, robbery and theft
And some thought it would be best
For that part of the court to stand
We did agree with heart and hand

At ten or twelve o'clock at night
There then began a bloody fight
Our men were crowded at the door
Forty or fifty if not more

All in an alley long and large
When twenty guns were all discharged
Upon the sons of liberty
So they should not go free

But the great God was our defense
There was non slain but William French
A pretty youth near twenty one
He was his father's loving son

But of the rest there are now five
That narrowly escaped with their lives
For they were wounded best or more
While French lay bleeding in his gore
—lines composed on the massacre at Westminster, March 13, 1775, by an
eyewitness who was wounded[83]

Sadly, the author of this song is unknown.

Chapter 5
Revolution

WESTMINSTER MINUTEMEN

The battles at Lexington and Concord took place on April 19. By late on April 20, word had reached Walpole, and probably Westminster's East Parish. The Walpole minutemen left for Cambridge the next morning. As far as we know, no East Parish men marched.

Word reached Putney and Westminster West the evening of Saturday, April 22. Early the next morning, Captain Abijah Moore started south with his company of minutemen. The company of thirty-five men included nine from Westminster, among them, according to family lore, fifteen-year-old William Crook Jr. Four of the nine were members of Azariah Wright's militia.[84]

Moore's company covered the 120 miles between Putney and Cambridge in three and a half days, crossing the Connecticut and many smaller rivers and streams, most unbridged and in full spring flood. They arrived to a tumultuous scene in Cambridge. Companies of minutemen had poured into the area. Some were returning home already, others were still arriving and the Continental army was being formed in the chaos.

Most Westminster men stayed and enlisted in the Continental army, receiving seven days' pay for their militia service. Gideon Badger and William Crook Sr. enlisted in Captain John Wood's company, Colonel Paul Dudley Sargent's regiment of Continental troops. John Abbey, John Wells, John Sweetland and Nathaniel Doubleday all enlisted in Captain Benjamin Hasting's company, Colonel Asa Whitcomb's Twenty-third Regiment. Badger was reported as having deserted Sargent's regiment on August 1,

1775, but had apparently just shifted over to Whitcomb's, where most of his fellow townsmen were serving. Others—Jabez Perry, John Wise and presumably young William Crook—went home after two weeks, receiving fourteen days' militia pay.

James Crawford of the West Parish heard of the battles one evening at sunset and departed before sunrise the next morning, independent of Moore's militia. He left behind a wife, an eleven-year-old son and a two-year-old daughter. Crawford likely joined the Continental army, though his name doesn't appear in record books. According to family tradition, he fought at Bunker Hill in June and returned home in late fall to help with the harvest. He spent the winter of 1775–76 with the Continental army.[85]

Clifford Chaffee and two of his brothers fought with Stark's New Hampshire regiment at Bunker Hill. Reuben Robinson is also said to have fought there.

POLITICAL CONSEQUENCES

On April 29, New York endorsed the Articles of Association in ringing terms—although not severing all ties with Britain or ending hopes of reconciliation.

> *We the Freemen, Freeholders and inhabitants of the City and County of New York, being greatly alarmed at the avowed design of the Ministry to raise a revenue in America, and shocked by the bloody scene now acting in the Massachusetts-Bay, do, in the most solemn manner, resolve never to be slaves; and do associate, under all ties of religion, honour, and love to our Country, to adopt and endeavour to carry into execution, whatever measures may be recommended by the Continental Congress…for the purpose of preserving our Constitution and opposing the execution of the several arbitrary and oppressive Acts of the British Parliament, until a reconciliation between Great Britain and America, on constitutional principles, (which we most ardently desire,) can be obtained.[86]*

The Revolution at this point was still cast as an effort to reform the mother country and return it to the honor and purity of its own principles.

This ambiguity was not apparently offensive to Cumberland County. A fifth convention, held at Westminster on June 6, passed the following resolves:

> *1. Resolved, nem. con., That the late Acts of the British Parliament, passed in order to raise a revenue in America, are unjust, illegal, and diametrically*

opposite to the Bill of Rights, and a fundamental principle of the British Constitution, which is "that no person shall have his property taken from him without his consent."

2. Resolved, nem. con., That we will resist and oppose the said Acts of Parliament, in conjunction with our brethren in America, at the expense of our lives and fortunes, to the last extremity, if our duty to God and our Country require the same.

3. Resolved, nem. con., That we think it needless to pass many resolves exhibiting our sentiments with regard to the unhappy controversy subsisting between Great Britain and America. Let it suffice, therefore, that we fully acquiesce with what our brethren have lately done at New York, in their late Association; and it is hereby resolved that the late Association entered into at New York is perfectly agreeable to the sentiments of the freeholders and inhabitants of this County, and that they fully acquiesce in the same.

4. Resolved, nem. con., That this County is at present in a very broken situation with regard to the civil authority. We therefore sincerely desire that the advice of the hounourable Congress may be by our Delegates transmitted to us, whereby some order and regularity may be established among us. We therefore should take it as a favour if the honourable Congress would particularly recommend to us in this County some measures to be pursued by us the inhabitants of the same; for we are persuaded that their advice herein would have great weight to influence our people universally to pursue such measures as would tend to the peace, safety, and good order of this County for the future.

5. Resolved, nem. con., That we, the inhabitants of this County, are at present in an extremely defenseless state with regard to arms and ammunition. We sincerely desire the honourable Provincial Congress would consider us in this respect, and from their generosity and goodness would do what in them lies for our relief in the premises. We have many brave soldiers, but unhappily for us, we have nothing to fight with.

They sent Colonel John Hazeltine, Dr. Paul Spooner and William Williams to New York to represent them.[87]

Ten days later came the Battle of Bunker Hill, the bloodiest single day of the Revolutionary War. The Continental army was defeated after a very tough fight, inflicting heavy casualties on the British and showing them that the war would not be easy or short. Eight men from Westminster fought there: those who marched with Abijah Moore, James Crawford and possibly Reuben Robinson. Many other Bunker Hill veterans would later settle in Westminster.

While battle rumbled to the south, civil disorder reigned back home. Cumberland County had overthrown New York civil authority and had only new organizations like the Committee of Safety to replace it.

We don't know how soon William Willard returned home after his release from prison, and there is no tradition of how he was received in Westminster. Others of the court party from other towns received a chilly welcome. Sabin and Wells were confined to their farms, and their neighbors were authorized to shoot them on sight if they strayed. Wells was rearrested by Leonard Spaulding at least once. We don't hear of any Westminster Yorkers receiving such treatment. Possibly, neighbors were more tolerant of one another. Compared with Dummerston, Rockingham or Brattleboro, the political climate in Westminster was flexible, tolerant, slippery or confusing, depending on your viewpoint.

Countywide, lawlessness and disputes continued. These were dealt with by the Committee of Safety. According to Chilton Williamson, the Committees of Safety were set up by Yorkists. Westminster's representatives until early 1777 were Elkanah Day, broadly Yorkist in his sympathies, and John Norton, a Tory. In contrast, Westminster's delegates to the county conventions, Joshua Webb and Nathaniel Robinson, were strong Whigs; the county convention was dominated by Whigs.

PROTEST AGAINST NORTON

In late 1775, the Provincial Congress of New York ordered county militias to be set up. The Cumberland County militia was divided into the Upper (northern) and Lower (southern) Regiments, and the Committee of Safety met on November 21 to choose officers. Of twenty-one delegates entitled to seats, only nine attended. They nominated seven of their number to military offices, including John Norton as first major.

Protest was immediate. Thirty-one Putney residents signed a letter sent to New York on December 6, noting, "The acts of this convention have discovered such a spirit of ignorance or tyranny, that we are apprehensive that our liberties, which we are contending for, are in danger, and like to be wrung out of our hands, by nine or ten arbitrary men." The nominated field officers had "an inimical spirit to the liberties of America."

Westminster followed on December 7 with a letter of its own, singling out John Norton and alleging that he had often disapproved of the proceedings of the colonies and was held in such disfavor that "neither in his own town, that of Westminster, nor in any other where he was known, could he obtain a majority of votes…for any office in the American service."[88] Fifty-six Dummerston residents signed a similar letter, referring to Norton as "universally known to be in opposition to the plan of liberty."[89]

The Provincial Congress did not approve the field officers for the Lower Regiment and wrote a letter to Cumberland County pleading for unity. After some negotiation, new officers were approved by a more public process on February 26, 1776. Westminster's Abijah Lovejoy, a Whig, was named second major.

The Lower Regiment consisted of six companies based in various towns. The Westminster Company was headed by Captain John Averill. Jabez Perry was first lieutenant, Azariah Wright was second lieutenant and William Crook was ensign. All were good, safe Whigs.

John Norton retained his seat on the Committee of Safety, dealing with matters of local justice and land disputes. They also chose men to represent Cumberland County in the New York Provincial Congress: Deacon John Sessions and Dr. Elkanah Day were among three chosen. Sessions, a well-liked early settler, was a committed Yorkist at this period, as was Day, relatively new in Westminster.

The committee also dealt with a letter written by Charles Phelps of Marlborough. For most of his life a loyal Yorker, in 1775 Phelps advocated Vermont's annexation to Massachusetts Bay. Many committee members favored the idea and wrote a letter to that effect to the New York Provincial Congress. Once the letter was written, Westminster members John Norton and Elkanah Day, along with John Bridgman of Hinsdale, opposed it.

WESTMINSTER MEN TO QUEBEC

In late 1775, Ethan Allen mounted a disastrous campaign to take the city of Montreal. It failed, and he was captured. Azariah Wright may have been with Allen, or he may have been with a small force of twelve men that went to the relief of Benedict Arnold, trekking through Maine in an attempt to take Quebec. Both attacks were ill planned and desperate, with Vermonters dying of hunger, cold and disease. Nothing is known about Wright's role, beyond his going to Canada, where "he and others were obliged to chew the leather of their pouches and cartridge boxes to obtain a little sustenance. He never fully recovered from the effects of his privations."[90]

According to family tradition, Reuben Robinson served under Colonel Enos in Benedict Arnold's expedition. This late-year trek through Maine ran into bad weather, and there were not enough provisions. Arnold pushed ahead with the better-equipped soldiers and most of the provisions, arriving at Quebec exhausted and too late. The troops under Colonel Enos struggled along behind until they and their provisions were completely exhausted. Then Enos disbanded his men and told them to get back to Boston if possible.

> *Reuben Robinson, who was in the rear guard, immediately set out for home. No one knows what route he followed…He was given no provision and if he had a musket, it was undoubtedly left along the trail as he soon became too exhausted to carry so heavy a weapon.*
>
> *He lived on berries and roots and drank from the clear mountain streams. Even if he could have shot game by the way, a fire would be almost impossible and time would be lost. He slept when his strength gave out huddled beside a tree or under a sheltering rock. He arrived home in about ten days—poor, starved, ragged and exhausted.*[91]

CREAN BRUSH AFTER LEXINGTON

Crean Brush's world turned upside down in 1775. The New York General Assembly, to which he had schemed to be elected, simply ceased to exist after Lexington and Concord. His property was marooned in hostile territory in upstate New York, New Hampshire and the Grants. Much of his lands and most of his personal property were in Westminster.

Fanny and Margaret joined Brush in New York after the outbreak of the Revolution.[92] Bryan says they "entrusted the valuables of the house to friends in New Hampshire." A New Hampshire resident, perhaps the same friend, owned the house briefly, and then it was occupied for some years by Dr. Elkanah Day.

Brush spent the summer in the city of New York, where he married off Fanny, supposedly to Captain John Buchanon, a British officer distantly connected to the wealthy shipping family of that name; Thomas Buchanon, head of the shipping firm, had land dealings with Brush in Vermont. No marriage document has been found for this wedding. While fifteen-year-old William Crook Jr. marched to war and back to Westminster again without receiving a scratch, Fanny Montusan, also fifteen, cried the whole day of her wedding and soon, according to family tradition, conceived a son.[93]

The boy was supposedly named John and was not raised by Fanny, who lost her husband within a year. According to family tradition, he died in battle; again, there's no evidence, and Bryan notes, "It was a frequent occurrence that marriages were mysteriously ended during the revolution when the spouses found themselves on opposite sides. It was a tumultuous time and one could hide bigamy in the frequent burnings of records."

The marriage may have been an attempt to place Fanny under the protection of the Buchanons while Brush was elsewhere. Early in the fall of 1775, he went to British-occupied Boston and offered his services to General Gage. As always, Brush had an ulterior motive or two. He quickly got a commission authorizing him to receive and protect the personal property of Bostonians in whose houses the British army would be quartered that winter. He was to care for the goods and return them when called upon, and he would be paid ten shillings a day.

Well enough, but Brush had another idea. In January he wrote to Gage, who had been ordered back to England, with this proposal: that he raise a body of three hundred volunteers plus officers and occupy "proper Posts on Connecticut River." Undoubtedly, one of those posts would have been rebellious Westminster. This, he said, would be "absolutely necessary for the purpose of reducing to Obedience, and bringing to Justice, a dangerous Gang of Lawless Banditti who…in open defiance of Government, holding themselves ameniable to no Law…have for many Years commited the most unheard of Cruelties and spread Terror and Destruction around them." This looks like a reference to the Green Mountain Boys, but by claiming that these banditti possessed territory "between the Connecticut River on the East and the Waters of Hudson's River," Brush included his old Westminster neighbors.

The British, however, had another job for Crean Brush. Gage had wanted to winter the army in Boston, but the Continental army was too threatening. The new British commander, General Howe, decided to evacuate. By February 1776, Brush had a large store of household goods and merchandise under his "protection." He obtained from Howe the power to seize more and began having the goods stowed on the brigantine *Elizabeth*.

He soon was breaking into shops and removing thousands of pounds worth of goods. He had been authorized to seize linens and woolens, considered helpful to the rebel army. But Brush took everything that wasn't nailed down, including the contents of private homes. He worked hard at his larceny, writing, "I solemnly aver, that from the 5th to the 13th of March, my own assiduity was so great that I did not in any one night allow myself more than two hours sleep."

The *Elizabeth* evacuated with the British army on March 17, with goods on board worth £20,000. By March 29, it was sailing north under convoy for Halifax, Nova Scotia. But the heavily laden ship fell behind the convoy and was captured off the coast of New Hampshire, with Crean Brush on board.

Brush was jailed in Massachusetts in solitary confinement, denied the use of pen, ink, paper or candles and forbidden to speak with anyone but the jailer. An unfinished letter found among his papers was published in the *Boston Gazette* so that, as the editors wrote, "the good people of these colonies may see the unwearied attempts of our implacable enemies to enslave them." In his letter, Brush advocated invading the colonies through Canada and made a special pitch for seizing "the River Connecticut—an object of the greatest consequence, as it forms the granary of Massachusetts Bay and Connecticut." His letter broke off just as his imagined expedition reached what must have been his personal goal—"the settled townships on Connecticut River," i.e., Westminster.

That was as close as Brush would ever get to his old hometown, but he didn't know that yet. He spent the next year and a half in prison, where according to tradition "he would often beguile his leisure hours by an undue indulgence in strong liquors."[94] Apparently he could get these in prison but not the more dangerous pen, ink and paper.[95]

WESTMINSTER: BIRTHPLACE OF NEW CONNECTICUT

On a parallel track with the American Revolution, Vermont moved toward separation from New York. Though the courts had been dissolved, the Westminster Courthouse remained the natural center of power in Cumberland County and was the stage on which much of the drama played out.

The Westminster Massacre had drawn the east and west sides of the Grants together. The Green Mountain Boys came to help Cumberland County at a time when many residents felt under assault by their own government. That gave the Allens greater influence. Easterners, in the light of their own experience, could see that westerners might have a point about New York, and the westerners pushed that connection, making, as Cadwallader Colden had predicted, "common cause."

Within Westminster, ambiguity prevailed. Some prominent residents were Tories and Yorkists (John Norton); some were Whigs and Yorkists (Elkanah Day, John Sessions, Medad Wright and Michael Gilson); and some were thoroughly for independence from both Britain and New York (Joshua Webb, Nathaniel Robinson and Azariah Wright). All political stripes continued to hold office and the respect of their fellow townspeople through changes of government and sometimes of their own opinions. Family relationships spanned the spectrum as well. Norton and Medad Wright were brothers-in-law; Azariah and Medad Wright were brothers. All three were next-door neighbors; their multitudes of children, all cousins, attended the log school and played together. Life must have been very complicated.

MORE CONVENTIONS

A convention at Dorset in January 1776 sent Heman Allen to petition the Continental Congress requesting that the Grants be recognized as independent from New York military authority. Congress considered the proposal flawed, as it lacked support from Cumberland County. They cited a letter from three Cumberland County militia officers that had promised "with the utmost cheerfulness and alacrity, to unsheath the sword in defence of the lives and properties of the good people" of the "ancient and truly respectable patriotick colony of New York."[96] Allen was told that independence was not feasible until the inhabitants could achieve unity.[97]

Thus, in the summer of 1776, the southwestern delegates met with the Committees of Safety of Cumberland and Gloucester Counties, seeking support for independence for the Grants. Eight self-appointed Cumberland County delegates attended a third Dorset convention in September 1776, with Joshua Webb and Nathaniel Robinson representing Westminster. This convention took several strong steps toward independence—one, rather charmingly naïve, was to write a letter to New York "to know if they have any objection against our being a Separate State from them."[98] Among the most detailed work they did was to set up a board of war and make decisions about how the militia would be governed in an independent Grants.

The west side members were expected to get the signatures of every male over the age of sixteen to the Dorset compact or (quite literally) know the reason why. East siders, reflecting political reality, were to notify their towns. Nathaniel Robinson was chosen to notify Westminster.

The next session of this body met at Westminster on October 30, 1776. Attendance was small; there had been British threats to Ticonderoga, the militia had been called out and the convention believed it improper to proceed. Webb and Robinson again represented Westminster. Elkanah Day was invited to sit with the convention as an observer (perhaps in an attempt to co-opt him), and Abijah Lovejoy was named to the committee to carry the petition to towns. Lovejoy died two months later, at age thirty-nine.

INDEPENDENCE DECLARED AT WESTMINSTER

The convention met again at the Westminster Courthouse on January 15, 1777. Twenty-two people attended, representing sixteen towns. Pomfret, Barnard and Royalton sent letters voting for a new state. Again, Robinson and Webb represented Westminster.

First the group examined the vote. "We find by examination that more than three-fourths of the people in Cumberland and Gloucester counties, that have acted, are for a new state; the rest we view as neuters." "That have acted" is the sleeper here; pro–New York towns like Brattleboro and Guilford sent no delegates to Dorset and did not vote.

Nonetheless, the convention voted, in its sixth item, "that the district of land commonly called and known by the name of New-Hampshire Grants,

The courtroom where court officials crafted the earliest version of the Massacre. French's inquest was held here, and this was also where Vermont declared independence and Stephen R. Bradley tried his first Vermont case. *Metros model, Westminster Historical Society.*

be a new and separate state; and for the future conduct themselves as such."
Then it recessed to write a declaration of independence.

The convention lacked a Thomas Jefferson. Its words would not ring through history, and perhaps because of this, Westminster is not remembered as "the birthplace of Vermont." But it was in Westminster Courthouse, stained with the blood of French and Houghton, that Vermont came into being.

DECLARATION OF INDEPENDENCE

To the hon^{ble} convention of representatives from the several towns on the west and east side of the range of Green Mountains, within the New Hampshire Grants, in convention assembled;

Your committee, to whom was referred the form of a declaration setting forth the right the inhabitants of said New Hampshire Grants have to form themselves into a separate and independent state, or government, beg leave to report viz;

RIGHT 1. That whenever protection is withheld, no alligiance is due or can of right be demanded.

2nd. That whenever the lives and properties of a part of a community have been manifestly aimed at by either the legislative or executive authority of such community, necessity requires a separation. Your committee are of opinion that the foregoing has, for many years past, been the conduct of the monopolizing land traders of the colony of New York; and that they have been not only countenanced, but encouraged, by both the legislative and executive authorities of the said state or colony. Many overt acts, in evidence of this truth, are so fresh in the minds of the members, that it would be needless to name them.

And whereas the Congress of the several states did, in said Congress, on the fifteenth of May A.D. 1776, in a similar case, pass the following resolution, viz. "Resolved, That it be recommended to the respective assemblies and conventions of the United Colonies, where no government sufficient to the exigencies of their affairs hath been hitherto establithsd, to adopt such government, as shall, in the opinion of the representatives of the people, best conduce to the happiness and saffety of their constituents in particular and America in general,"—Your committee, having duly deliberated on the continued conduct of the authority of New York, before recited, and on the equitableness on which the aforesaid resolution of

Congress was founded, and considering that a just right exists in this people to adopt measures for their own security, not only to enable them to secure their rights against the usurpations of Great-Britain, but also against that of New York, and the several other governments claiming jurisdiction of this territory, do offer the following declaration, viz.:

This Convention, whose members are duly chosen by the free voice of their constituents in the several towns, on the New-Hampshire Grants, in public meeting assembled, in our own names, and in behalf of our constituents, do hereby proclaim and publicly declare that the district of territory comprehending and usually known by the name and description of the New Hampshire Grants, of right ought to be, and is herby declared forever hereafter to be considered as a separate, free and independent jurisdiction or state; by the name and forever hereafter to be called, known and distinguished by the name of NEW CONNECTICUT; [crossed out; the words "alias Vermont" are inserted here] *and that the inhabitants that at present are, or that hereafter may become resident, either by procreation or emigration, within said territory, shall be entitled to the same privileges, immunities and enfranchisements as are allowed; and on such condition, and in the same manner, as the present inhabitants in future shall or may enjoy; which are, and forever shall be considered, to be such privileges and immunities to the free citizens and denizens as are, or, at any time hereafter, may be allowed to any such inhabitants of any of the free and independent states of America: And that such privileges and immunities shall be regulated in a bill of rights, and by a form of government, to be established in the next adjourned session of this convention.*[99]

(A few months after New Connecticut declared its independence at Westminster, it was found that a place in Pennsylvania had already claimed that name. At that time—before the convention at Windsor in July 1777—it was decided to change the name to Vermont. The manuscript of the declaration was altered; the words "alias Vermont" were written in next to New Connecticut. This was not part of the original document.)

The convention voted to accept this report. Joshua Webb was named to the Committee of War and to a committee to raise $100 to defray the cost of delegates' expenses for going to the Continental Congress. It also drew up a letter forbidding the current Cumberland County delegates (including John Sessions) from sitting in the Provincial Congress of New York.

LETTER AS PER NINETEENTH VOTE

Gentlemen:—The General Convention consisting of Delegates from the several Counties and Towns known by the name of the New Hampshire Grants have met according to adjournment at Westminster the 16th inst., and have resolved and declared the above District of Land shall hereafter be a distinct State or Government, and the Inhabitants therof have full authority to make such laws as they shall from time to time think fit.

The said Convention therefore desire and request that you will on sight hereof withdraw yourselves from the Convention of the State of New York, and appear there no more in the character of Representatives for the County of Cumberland; as you were not chosen by a Majority of the people at large.

Gentleman I am your most obedient
Hum^{ble} Servant,
Ebenezer Hoisington, Chairman Sub-Committee[100]

Sessions, along with Colonel Joseph Marsh and Simon Stevens, Esq., had been appointed by the Cumberland County Committee of Safety, not by the people. Sessions returned for the session of August 18, 1779, along with Elkanah Day and Micah Townshend.

THE PRESS RELEASE

A revised declaration of independence was prepared for the press by Captain Heman Allen, Colonel Thomas Chandler and Nathan Clark, Esq. Considerably less clotted in its language, it was disapproved by the convention of June 4 because it didn't list causes for seeking independence from New York.

The press version declared:

In Convention of the representatives from the several counties and towns of the New Hampshire Grants, holden at Westminster, January 15, 1777, by adjournment.

Whereas the Honorable the Continental Congress did on the 4th day of July last, declare the United Colonies in America to be free and independent of the crown of Great Britain; which declaration we most cordially acquiesce in: And whereas by the said declaration the arbitrary acts of the crown are null and void, in America, consequently the jurisdiction by said crown granted to New York government over the people of the New-Hampshire Grants is totally dissolved:

We therefore, the inhabitants, on said tract of land, are at present without law or government, and may be truly said to be in a state of nature; consequently a right remains to the people of the said Grants to form a government best suited to secure their property, well being and happiness. We the delegates from the several counties and towns on said tract of land, bounded as follows: South on the North line of Massachusetts Bay; East on Connecticut River; North on Canada line; West as far as the New Hampshire Grants extends:

After several adjournments for the purpose of forming ourselves into a distinct separate state, being assembled at Westminster, do make and publish the following Declaration, viz.:

"That we will, at all times hereafter, consider ourselves as a free and independent state, capable of regulating our internal police, in all and every respect whatsoever—and that the people on said Grants have the sole and exclusive and inherent right of ruling and governing themselves in such manner and form as in their own wisdom they shall think proper, not inconsistent or repugnant to any resolve of the Honorable Continental Congress.

"Furthermore, we declare by all the ties which are held sacred among men, that we will firmly stand by and support one another in this our declaration of a state, and in endeavoring as much as in us lies, to suppress all unlawful routs and disturbances whatever. Also we will endeavor to secure to every individual his life, peace and property against all unlawful invaders of the same.

"Lastly we hereby declare, that we are at all times ready, in conjunction with our brethren in the United States of America, to do our full proportion in maintaining the just war against the tyrannical invasions of the ministerial fleets and armies, as well as any other foreign enemies, sent with express purpose to murder our fellow brethren, and with fire and sword to ravage our defenceless country.

"The said state hereafter to be called by the name of NEW CONNECTICUT."
Extract from the minutes.

Ira Allen, clerk[101]

The Vermont constitution was written at a convention in Windsor in 1777. Among the drafters was Bildad Andross, formerly of Westminster. Arrested after the Massacre, he supposedly became dissatisfied with the New York courts and their treatment of the court at Westminster and moved to Bradford in 1776. He became a supporter of the American Revolution.[102]

THE BRITISH ARE COMING!

It's one thing to declare independence and another thing to make it stick. In January 1777, neither New Connecticut nor the United States of America looked like a sure bet. Benedict Arnold had won a decisive battle on Lake Champlain in 1776, but the lake remained a swift highway straight to the heart of the northern colonies. In early 1777, a British force of 7,500 men assembled in Canada under General John Burgoyne, planning to march to Albany, link with other troops and isolate New England from the rest of the colonies.

Burgoyne's force began moving in June 1777. By early July, it was threatening Ticonderoga, and a call went out for help. A letter from John Sessions to Medad Wright shows the level of alarm felt in Westminster when the word arrived:

John Sessions and especially Medad Wright are often called Tories, but in 1777, they responded to the call for troops to defend Fort Ticonderoga. *Photo by Ed Sawyer, from Sawyer family collection.*

Westminster July 8ᵗʰ 1777
Sir

I this moment received a letter from major painter who wrote in consequence of orders from the general at ticonderoga, informing that there is an attack at that place etc—these are to request you to call this Town together and order every effective man to appear at our meetinghouse at one o clock this Day with arms etc in order to March to Tye. Warn all as far a Barney broock and to west I will warn the west at our end of the Town I am in haist your humble Servnt

John Sessions[103]

Sessions couldn't know that Ticonderoga had already been abandoned and that Seth Warner's Green Mountain Regiment had fought a rear-guard action at Hubbardton that stopped the British pursuit and allowed American troops to regroup. Presumably, word of those actions reached Westminster before they could "March to Tye."

The heart of Vermont was now threatened, and Cumberland County responded, organizing into guard companies and scouting parties. There was fear that Burgoyne meant to lay waste to the Connecticut River Valley, and that fear was fully justified.

THE SARATOGA CAMPAIGN

On July 19, New Hampshire's John Stark was ordered to take command of Fort Number 4 in Charlestown, with one-quarter of the New Hampshire militia. He gathered more men from surrounding Vermont and New Hampshire towns, sending them west to Seth Warner as quickly as they could be supplied with kettles, rum and bullets.

According to Holden family tradition, Francis and Charles Holden joined Stark's army as it passed. Though the main army marched through Chester, Andover and Peru, other units headed to Bennington by a more southerly route. By tradition, a military road leads from the Connecticut River across the southern part of Westminster, passing very near the Holden homesteads. Parts of this road are still visible.

On August 9, in order to "try the affections of the country, disconcert the councils of the enemy, and obtain large supplies of cattle, horses, and carriages," Burgoyne ordered Lieutenant Colonel Baum to march from Battenkill through Manchester and over the mountains to Rockingham, sending Mohawk fighters and light troops upriver while taking his main force downriver to Brattleboro and back across to Albany. This would have meant substantial life and property loss for Westminster, which lay on Baum's proposed line of march.

But on August 16, John Stark's 1,800 men attacked Baum's German mercenaries six miles northwest of Bennington. It was a fierce battle; Stark described the firing as "like a continuous clap of thunder." According to *History of Rockingham*, "Men at work in their fields both in Rockingham and Walpole distinctly heard the sound of the cannonading." The people of Westminster would have heard it too, especially the Holden wives and children up on Windmill Hill.

Generals Stark and Warner routed Burgoyne's German troops at Bennington. Burgoyne lost two hundred men killed and seven hundred taken prisoner, one-tenth of his army. The Battle of Bennington restored American morale; just as important, it crippled Burgoyne. However, the British army remained a threat, and more American troops were needed.

On August 29, twelve Westminster men enlisted for forty days in Captain John Petty's company of Williams's regiment (* indicate members of Azariah Wright's militia):

Simeon Burke*	Seth Gould (Goold)*
James Crawford	Samuel Phippen*
William Perry	Ichabod Ide Jr.*
William Crook*	Sylvanus Fisk
Nathaniel Robertson (Robinson)	Atherton Chaffee Jr.*
William Eaton	William Gould*[104]

Other Westminster men enlisted in Moses Johnson's regiment from September 25 to October 17:

Asa Averel (Averill)	Nehemiah McNeal (McNeil)
John Abbe*	John McNeal (McNeil)
Abraham Dickerson (Dickinson)	Charles Rice
Israel Ide*	Ichabod Ide Sr.
James Ide[105]	

Still more Westminster men served in New Hampshire regiments during the time of the Saratoga Campaign:

First New Hampshire Regiment
Jonathan Fuller*
Moses Goold

Nehemiah Goold
Other regiments
Uriah Carpenter (Captain Griggs's company)
Eliphat Shipman (Captain Griff's company)
Abner Wise (Colonel Scammel's regiment)[106]

SILVER BUCKLES, SILVER SPOONS

Meanwhile, the war came to Westminster.

It's late August 1777, and Rhoda Harlow is walking out to the field to get sweet corn for supper. A week or two ago it was possible to hear the sound of artillery, like distant thunder, from the battle being fought near Bennington. Now there's only birdsong, the grunting of hogs and the shouts of children playing. To the thirty-year-old wife and mother, distant battles seem less important than getting supper on the table.

But what's that bright red patch deep in the corn? Has she been thinking too much about redcoats? Because surely there can't be one here.

But according to family tradition, there was a redcoat—a British officer, in fact—lying wounded in the Harlows' field at the top of Courthouse Hill. Injured at Bennington, he was probably being marched to Massachusetts with other prisoners when he escaped, planning to travel upriver to Canada. In the Harlow field he gave out, within sight of John Norton's Tory Tavern and the Westminster jail, courthouse and whipping post.

Perhaps he had a winning personality. Perhaps Rhoda Harlow believed in Christian mercy. The Harlows weren't particularly partisan; the name simply doesn't turn up in military records of the time. For whatever reason, Rhoda took the wounded man into the house, hid him and nursed him until he was recovered, about three months. When he was well enough to travel, he was smuggled north to Canada. No one outside the immediate family knew of his presence—a necessary precaution as Rhoda's brother, Philip Alexander, was a Green Mountain Boy.

When he left, the officer gave his silver shoe buckles to Rhoda; probably they were the only thing of value he had with which to express his gratitude to the woman who saved his life and freedom. According to family tradition, the British officer returned to America on a visit around 1819 and came up to Vermont to visit the Harlows; Rhoda died about three years before he returned.

Rhoda's daughter Annis married Zacheas Cole, a Dummerston-born silversmith, in 1815. He was her second husband and six years her junior.

One of the five spoons made in Westminster from a British officer's silver shoe buckles. The Harlows hid the escaped officer and helped him flee to Canada. *Vermont Historical Society.*

Cole made five silver spoons from the officer's shoe buckles, one for each of his and Annis's daughters. One of the spoons was donated to the Vermont Historical Society by Perley Farnum Richmond, a great-granddaughter of Zacheas and Annis Cole, in 1957.[107]

Westminster Drummer Killed

While a British officer sheltered in the Harlow home, Westminster men saw action in the Saratoga Campaign, as American forces first blocked Burgoyne from marching south to Albany and then cut his supply lines, driving him deep into a trap from which there was no escape. The fiercest battles of the campaign took place at Freeman's Farm, between Bemis Heights and Saratoga. The first came on September 19, an unseasonably hot fall day. The three New Hampshire regiments bore the brunt of extremely heavy fighting, facing off against three companies of British foot soldiers as well as German and British artillery. Among those killed was a drummer in the First New Hampshire Regiment, Jonathan Fuller of Westminster. A member of Azariah Wright's militia, Fuller lived in the West Parish near the present

Ranney-Crawford house. His age is unknown; his father was supposedly a soldier in the Revolution as well. So far as we know, Jonathan Fuller was the only Westminster man killed in battle in the Revolutionary War. He was likely buried near where he fell in a mass grave; single graves were reserved for officers and, in a bloody battle like Freeman's Farm, for mid- and upper-level officers at that.

Petty's and Johnson's men were also available for combat and may have fought at Freeman's Farm. The terms of enlistment for Petty's men ran out before Burgoyne's surrender on October 18. Johnson's men were enlisted until October 17. On that date, the two armies were in surrender negotiations.

The New Hampshire regiments stayed with the Continental army through Valley Forge and beyond. Moses Gold (Goold) a private, Westminster, is listed in Vermont records as wounded in November 1777. This may have been during a mutiny while the regiment camped near Fishkill, New York, in which a captain and a private lost their lives. Goold died of wounds on January 10, 1778. He is not buried in Westminster; if he stayed with his regiment, he would have been at Valley Forge.

Nehemiah Goold survived the winter at Valley Forge but died, probably of disease, on August 10, 1778. The army was then camped at White Plains, New York.

JAILBREAK

In January 1777, as New Connecticut was born in Westminster, Margaret Brush arrived in Boston and began to visit her imprisoned husband frequently. There's some evidence that by August, Brush had been tried on three indictments resulting from his plundering and possibly acquitted. However, he was not released.

Margaret visited again on November 5 and stayed for several hours. When it was time for the prisoners to be locked up for the night, the turnkey opened the door and watched as a tall figure in a dress walked past him into the darkness. The next morning, when the turnkey opened the loophole to pass in the breakfast tray, there was no response. He called several times, and eventually a woman's voice answered. "I am not Mr. Brush's keeper."

Crean Brush had escaped; Margaret had apparently worn two dresses and given one to her husband. Bryan speculates that her friend (later, her husband) Patrick Wall, a tailor, may have sewn her a special outfit. But Margaret carried out her plan alone and refused to say a word about her husband's whereabouts. He mounted the horse she had left tied for him and made his way to New York.

There he worked hard to recover his property, especially his lands in the Grants. This was made difficult because Ira Allen, treasurer of the fledgling state, had decided to fund the militia by confiscating the property of Tories, of whom Brush was eminently one. The commissioners of sequestration were appointed on July 28, 1777, following the evacuation of Ticonderoga and the Battle of Hubbardton. Brush's old neighbor Nathaniel Robinson was on the commission.

Early the following spring, frustrated and despairing, Brush apparently killed himself. Accounts differ; one tradition has him cutting his throat in a lawyer's office. Another, published in a Boston paper at the time, has him shooting himself in his own chambers, after he had "applied to the [Loyalist] Commander there, for a Consideration of the Insults and, as he told the Story, the many Losses &c. he met while here, when he received for Answer 'Your Conduct merited them, and more,' which so enraged him that he retired to his Chamber, where, with a Pistol, he besmeared the Room with his Brains."[108] It's also possible that he was murdered. Brush was a much hated man, and according to family lore, he had just ordered wood to heat his room—not the action of a man about to kill himself.

Whatever the mechanism, Crean Brush was dead. His ambition and effort had helped make Westminster politically important. The people and property he left behind would continue to affect the town for years to come.

"Terrifyed with Threats"

The Saratoga Campaign produced a tremendous victory when America needed one badly. At least twenty-one Westminster men helped achieve that victory. But with Burgoyne defeated, the war shifted south again, and Vermont returned to preoccupation with its other revolution.

There was now, in theory, a new government, that of the state of Vermont. However, the institutions of New York government continued, though with gradually diminishing attendance and authority. The political situation was beyond complex. There were "Tories," "Yorkers" and "Vermonters"; there were pro- and anti-Allen factions within the Vermonters' side. Many towns, including Westminster, remained deeply divided.

Captain Michael Gilson and Nathaniel Robinson were Westminster's members on the Cumberland County Committee of Safety in 1777.

Robinson, a strong Whig in favor of independence from New York, did not attend the meetings. Gilson, also a Whig, consistently favored New York government. He signed onto a Committee of Safety report dated June 26, 1777, from Brattleboro; the meeting had adjourned there after being "terrifyed with threats from the people who are Setting up a new State here."

The committee deplored the proceedings at Windsor, where a Vermont constitution had been adopted, and complained about the state of affairs in Cumberland County and their distrust of their fellow citizens. "We Really Beleave that the Leaders of the people who are for a new State in this County are persuing that which they Esteem their privit Interest and prefer that to the publick weal of America."[109] The Committee of Safety meeting at Westminster on September 2, 1777, was attended by only nine members out of twenty-one and appears to have been the last.

JOHN SESSIONS'S LETTER

The setting up of a Vermont government went on apace. A letter from John Sessions to John McKesson, Esq., secretary of the New York Provincial Congress (or Convention), dated two days after the final Committee of Safety meeting, signals both his commitment to New York and the likelihood that he would soon have to "give up the Point."

Sessions stresses that he's always been open about his opinions—"Honesty is the best Polacy"—and that he's paid for that. His warm, moderate, flexible character shines through in the following letter, despite the absence of punctuation and the sometimes unusual spelling:

Westminster 4ᵗʰ Septemʳ 1777

> *Sir it gave me Peculiar Satisfaction when I found not only by your Letter but by the Resolves you therein mentioned that our affairs have ben upon the Carpet in Congress—but it by no means answers the end (at Present) to stop the Progress of the faction respecting a New State I would have sent you one of the Connecticut Papers wherein is contained the Construction these People Put upon the Resolves of Congress, but I conclude you have seen it so that will be kneedless—if they had Resolved they would break their necks if they Did not Desist I Dont know but those People might have thought they were in arenest but the Honᵇˡᵉ Congress and Council of this State wil become more Sencable (I trust) of the Temper and Disposition*

that actuates those People than they have ben and I am sorry they hant before now if it had been supprest sooner it in all Probability might have ben Effectual but the Event now I am unable fully to Determine altho I can Conjecture & is what I should Dread—my opposition has rendred my Situation Somewhat unhappy at present but trust shall find the old Maxim True in the end—(viz) Honesty is the best Polacy I have ben a Sort of a Micaiah in the affair & I believe many would be glad I were in house of Jonathan & have reason to expect this will be my fait if sumthing is not Done Soone shall be obliged to give up the Point—as to News I have nothing special to Write only it is a very sickly time among us and in Neighbouring Towns. Should be glad of a Line from you whereby I may understand what your Sentemon are abought our affairs as I want to act with safety and Prudence both for my Self State and Country.

Sir I am with Due respect
your most obedient ser[nt]
John Sessions[110]

Within six years, Sessions would be chief judge of the Windham County Court, and by 1787, he was Westminster's representative in the Vermont legislature. There were people whose loyalty to New York was undying, but John Sessions was one who could move on.

COUNTERREVOLUTION

In 1778, several meetings were held in southern Vermont to express support for remaining in New York. Brattleboro voted to denounce the Vermont General Assembly's actions for "disunit[ing] the friends of America in this important contest with Great Britain."[111] Practically, Brattleboro doubted that Vermont had the monetary wherewithal or the necessary skills to establish a state—a valid point when we remember that at the time of the Massacre Brattleboro had boasted exactly one lawyer. Other town committees signed onto the protest, including Westminster's. While certainly not the sentiment of the whole town, it was the sentiment of an influential faction.

The legislature took little notice. It was busy playing with counties. Cumberland and Gloucester Counties were combined into one enormous entity, Unity County. Four days later, the name was changed to Cumberland. Three days after that, Cumberland was divided again into two shires, the upper called Newbury and the lower Westminster. Briefly, Westminster was a county as well as a town.

AN UNSCIENTIFIC SURVEY

In the spring, Vermont raised troops in Cumberland County. This created further friction with the Yorkist Whigs, who were happy to support America's revolution but not Vermont's. Petitions to Governor Clinton of New York met with encouraging words, and a poll was done in southern Cumberland County—by methods unknown—to see if the majority of voters supported New York or Vermont. Westminster, Hinsdale, Guilford, Halifax, Brattleboro, Fulham (Dummerston), Newfane, Putney, Springfield, Weathersfield and Draper were polled.

The committees reported the following results:

480 voters supported New York

320 voters supported Vermont

185 voters were neutral (or neuter, according to the exact wording)[112]

According to the committee's report, "Westminster sent no Return; is about equally divided—the number of voters for New York about 40." The population of Westminster was likely over one thousand at this time, probably a quarter being men of voting age. Forty votes for New York doesn't at all sound like an equal division.[113]

During this period, sixteen New Hampshire towns were briefly annexed to Vermont, in part to counter the power of the western towns and the Allens. Courts were reestablished at Newbury and Westminster, with jurisdiction over the adjacent New Hampshire towns. This lasted until February, when the legislature hastily withdrew from the Eastern Union in response to the extreme displeasure of Congress.

CONFISCATIONS

In February 1779, the Vermont legislature voted to confiscate the estates of Vermont Tories. Major Thomas Chandler Jr., son of the infamous judge Chandler who precipitated the Massacre, was commissioner for the sale of Westminster estates. His jurisdiction included Rockingham and Chester, too, but Westminster was the plum, containing the estates of Billy Paterson and Crean Brush. Brush's holdings in Westminster amounted to five or six thousand acres. The politically nimble John Norton, though always known as a Tory, was not targeted, perhaps because he was a friend of Ethan Allen's.

The confiscations became a bit of a free-for-all. Leonard Spaulding of Dummerston simply took possession of the Governor's Meadow at

Westminster, as well as two Westminster lots and a barn, all owned by Crean Brush. In response to this and other abuses, the Governor's Council took Brush's estate out of the hands of the commissioners of sequestration and gave charge of it to Nathaniel Robinson.

The legislature also voted to forbid the return of "all inimical persons" under pain of receiving twenty to forty lashes on the naked back. A list of people to whom this act applied included Crean Brush, already dead a year.[114]

BRUSH'S LAND DIVIDED

Stephen Rowe Bradley, a lawyer and politician who succeeded Brush in social and political position in Westminster, bought hundreds of acres of his land. Ethan Allen controlled and sold many parcels through his family connection with Brush's widow. John Norton also acquired much of the confiscated land. Bradley, Allen and Norton later sold the land, prospering as Brush had sought to prosper.

Other smaller operators also profited. William Crook, by quitclaim deed, gained title to "a certain mill place" in lot number 8 of the fifth range. This was near the end of the present Patch Road, soon to be known as Crook's Mills, where he and his brother established grist- and sawmills. Crook bought two other lots as well, 9 and 10 in the third range of eight-acre lots. Others who got Brush land included Nathan Fisk, the jailer, and William Hyde.

> *PETITION OF WILLIAM CROOK FOR "THE MILL LOT" IN WESTMINSTER*
> *That a Number of Inhabitants of the town of Westminster aforesaid Sometyime in the year 1774 bought of Robert Crooks in Said Westminster a mill place in the Eight Lot and fith Range of Lots…and Said Mill place was Deeded to Crean Brush who became obligated to have Grist Mill ready to run on the Said two acres in the Course of the ensuing Year for the benefit of Said town as by an obligation from Said Brush will appear and…Said Brush in the Course of Said Year instead of Building Said mill to Grind for Said town as agreed the resentment of his injured Countrymen fled for refuge to the Savage Britians thereby forfeiting the whole of his estate…*
> *Manchester 2 Day October 1779*[115]

Brush's personal property was scattered around Westminster. His clock, according to Hall, was still tolling the hours in 1858, though he doesn't mention in which home.[116]

Chapter 6
The Cow Wars

In the February 1779 session, the Vermont legislature set up new rules on service in the militia. Among other provisions, it imposed a fine of eighteen pounds for refusal of military service. Cash was scarce; militia captains were empowered to seize goods or chattel of soldiers refusing to serve Vermont and sell them at vendue. Some people felt that the new law was more about raising money than strengthening the militia.

In April, the Vermont Board of War ordered a levy of men for service. Prominent Putney Yorkers Captain James Clay and Lieutenant Benjamin Willson refused to serve, and on April 21, each had a cow seized by recruiting sergeant William McWain. The cows were to be sold at public auction in Putney on April 28.

The morning of the twenty-eighth, nearly one hundred unarmed men assembled in Putney. Most were members of Colonel Eleazer Patterson's militia regiment and were under his command. When they couldn't argue the Vermont sergeant into stopping the sale, they simply seized the cows and returned them to their owners.[117]

A few days later, on May 4, Yorker committees chosen in nine southeastern towns, including Westminster, convened at Brattleboro and petitioned New York governor Clinton for relief. According to a separate letter written by Colonel Patterson, opinion about "the pretended state of Vermont" was about equally divided in Rockingham and Westminster; this is the exact wording of the committee poll and is likely taken from it. Patterson's statement was probably exaggerated; we have no way of running an opinion poll at this late date. Patterson expressed a concern that efforts to recruit troops in Westminster and Rockingham would lead to "broils."

Clinton advised the Yorkers "in no instance to acknowledge the authority of Vermont, unless where there is no alternative left between submission and inevitable ruin." In case of violence in any of the Yorkist towns, he offered "all the assistance in my power" and urged everyone to wait patiently for Congress to resolve the matter.[118]

THE BLACK HOLE OF WESTMINSTER

On May 18, writs for the arrest of forty-four people involved in the cow rescue were signed by Ira Allen. Thirty-six were arrested, including many prominent men—Benjamin Butterfield and Micah Townshend of Brattleboro, Noah Sabin of Putney and Westminster's Elkanah Day, Michael Gilson, Medad Wright, Benjamin Whitney, Billy Willard, Joseph Willard, Bildad Easton, John Norton and Deacon John Sessions. Not arrested were Joseph Ide, Ichabod Ide Jr. and a Wilcox, possibly Ephraim, all from the West Parish. Perhaps the posse didn't loop through Westminster West.

The Westminster prisoners' social status was high, and they had given considerable service to their town, county and the state of New York. Sessions was a founding member of the church and one of its first deacons; he and Day, a popular doctor, had represented the county in the New York Convention for several terms. Gilson, Norton, Wright and the Willards had been prominent townsmen since 1760.

The other prisoners were also prominent, and many had excellent Whig credentials. Micah Townshend, a lawyer from Westchester, New York, had clerked the Committee of Safety there and commanded a company of militia in support of General Washington. He had moved to Brattleboro only the year before and married one of the daughters of the Tory Samuel Wells. A loyal Yorker in constant communication with Governor Clinton, Townshend was a man of great abilities who would one day be Vermont's secretary of state.

Noah Sabin was a judge, justice of the peace and Putney's town clerk. A committed Tory, he had been jailed following the Massacre, was absent from Vermont for a year and was then confined to his farm by the Committee of Safety on pain of death. Sabin was considered a man of uncommon mind and superior education. Hall notes of the prisoners, "They were generally men of note and influence, and among them were some of greater ability than those who were to pass judgement upon their conduct."[119]

Thirty-six eminent citizens of Cumberland County were imprisoned in this cell during the Cow Wars. French died here, as did Judge Thomas Chandler. *Dorothy Metros model, Westminster Historical Society.*

Nonetheless, all were jailed at Westminster. Hall says, "Closely crowded together in one room, the prisoners were obliged to remain standing on their feet during the first night of their confinement. This, and the excessive heat of the weather, rendered their sufferings most intolerable."[120] Conditions on the peaceful brow of Courthouse Hill in Westminster resembled the Black Hole of Calcutta or a Nazi rail car.

Fortunately, the period of acute misery was brief. The next day, the prisoners were made more comfortable, Hall says, "in answer to their just demands." There may also have been public outcry. The families of the Westminster men were all close by; Day, Wright and Norton could likely see their houses. It's easy to imagine that wives and children protested. It's also easy to imagine that one whiff of the cell the next morning might have brought the jailers to a sense of humane justice. Nathan Fisk of Westminster was the jail keeper at this time, and Westminster's Jesse Burk of Westminster was acting sheriff. They had known many of their prisoners for years.

In New York, Governor Clinton made noises. He planned to convene the state legislature in June, mentioned sending one thousand men to Brattleboro and promised provisions of beef and pork to Samuel Wells. None of this was forthcoming, but it did raise concern in Vermont. To protect the sheriff against attack from Yorkers, Governor Chittenden ordered Colonel Ethan Allen, Colonel Joseph Marsh and Colonel Samuel Fletcher to bring militia to Cumberland County for the sitting of the court. In a scene reminiscent of the Massacre, Westminster teemed with armed men during the week of the trial. Between 200 and 350 militiamen guarded the courthouse and patronized the taverns.

According to the Yorkers, Ethan Allen was boastful and abusive, assaulting and wounding several people with his sword "without the least provocation." The county committee convened in Brattleboro again on May 25 and sent another express to Governor Clinton informing him of the situation and requesting speedy help. They vowed that only their regard for human life prevented them from rescuing the prisoners; they didn't mention that they were substantially outnumbered. If they didn't get help, they said, "our persons and property must be at the disposal of Ethan Allen, which is more to be dreaded than death with all its terrors."[121]

BRIMSTONE

On May 26, eight days after the arrests, an adjourned session of superior court convened at Westminster, Moses Robinson of Bennington presiding. That day Westminster townsmen favorable to Vermont "forcibly seized the public stock of gunpowder"—one hundred pounds, stored in the courthouse—and placed twenty-five pounds of it in the hands of their friends. This, according to Hall, was "to guard against interruption during the session."[122]

The prisoners were marched upstairs and the legal preliminaries dealt with. A move for adjournment by the prisoners was denied, but they did procure council: one Stephen Rowe Bradley, a young Connecticut attorney and war veteran who had recently moved to Bennington.

Bradley succeeded in quashing several of the indictments. The trial of the remainder was about to proceed when Ethan Allen swaggered in, "accoutered in his military dress, with a large cocked hat on his head profusely ornamented with gold lace, and a sword of fabulous dimensions swinging at his side."

He proceeded to harangue Bradley and the state's attorney, Noah Smith, uttering one of his most famous lines: "I would have the young gentleman to know that with my logic and reasoning, from the eternal fitness of things, I can upset his Blackstones, his whitestones, his gravestones and his brimstones." He warned the judge against "this artful lawyer, Bradley," and the likelihood that the prisoners might escape justice and then stalked out of court.[123] The trial continued. The defendants pled not guilty, arguing that they were subjects of New York and had acted under that state's authority and also that as the Vermont law was new and had not been promulgated, they were essentially in ignorance. That argument was technically true but specious, since their action had been a protest against the very law of which they now claimed ignorance.

After hearing other witnesses, the judges found them guilty and imposed fines. The fines were relatively lenient, and soon thereafter Governor Chittenden issued a pardon proclamation drafted by Stephen R. Bradley.

STEPHEN ROWE BRADLEY COMES TO WESTMINSTER

Stephen Rowe Bradley was born in Wallingford, Connecticut, in 1754, the son of Moses and Mary Row Bradley. By tradition the Bradleys had been "Cromwell men and staunch dissenters."[124] The family had been in Connecticut since 1644 and were friends and fellow townsmen of Governor Theophilus Eaton.

During Bradley's senior year at Yale he prepared an almanac, and an edition of two thousand copies was published in 1774. After graduating in 1775, Bradley enlisted in and by January 1776 was captain of a company called the Cheshire Volunteers. In December 1776, with the rank of adjutant, he was made vendue-master and quartermaster. He was an aide-de-camp to General Wooster during the British attack on Danbury on April 27, 1777; Wooster was fatally wounded in that fight.[125]

Following that battle, Bradley returned to Yale, where he

Stephen Rowe Bradley litigated his first case in Westminster, defending a group of Yorkers. He became one of Vermont's first pair of U.S. senators. *Vermont Historical Society.*

received the degree AM in 1778. He came to Vermont to practice law in early 1779 and made his first Vermont court appearance in Westminster that May representing the Yorkists.

Bradley moved to Westminster later that year. As the most important town in the most populous county of Vermont, Westminster was the natural place for an ambitious lawyer to locate. Bradley bought a lot from the confiscated estate of Crean Brush and built a large house on the Upper Street, just below Courthouse Hill. Over the next few years it would serve as an inn for judges when court was in session and would host other important guests, including the future Fanny Allen.

Bradley Rises

Like Crean Brush, Stephen Rowe Bradley conveyed additional importance to Westminster by his political and military actions. In October 1779, he was named by Governor Chittenden to a five-member committee to present Vermont's claim of independence to Congress. (Other members were Ethan Allen, Jonas Fay, Paul Spooner and Moses Robinson.) Bradley, twenty-six, was the youngest member and the least familiar with the Vermont situation. The job of writing up Vermont's case was delegated to him, and he did it quite successfully. Bradley's pamphlet, "Vermont's Appeal to the Candid and Impartial World," was read before the Council of Vermont at Arlington on December 10, approved thereby and ordered to be published. In part, it read:

> *The State of Vermont, we have now clearly shown, has a natural right to independence—honor, justice and humanity forbid us tamely to surrender that freedom which our innocent posterity has a right to demand and receive from their ancestors…while we wear the name of Americans, we never will surrender those glorious privileges for which so many have fought, bled and died; we appeal to your own feelings, as men of like sufferings, whether you would submit your freedom and independence to the arbitrement of any court, or referees under heaven! If you would, after wasting so much blood and treasure, you are unworthy the names of Americans: if you would not, condemn not others in what you allow yourself.*[126]

On the strength of these words, Bradley was chosen on February 1, 1780, to represent Vermont at the current session of Congress. He laid Vermont's appeal before Congress but had no opportunity to appear before any committee.

Bradley also represented Westminster in the General Assembly, which met in Westminster that March. He was appointed to a three-person committee to look into why some residents of Cumberland County were opposed to the authority of Vermont. Bradley was unable to make any headway, despite all his political talents; opposition in Guilford and Halifax, the most populous towns in the county, was particularly serious.

LIBEL (AND RACISM?)

The passions of the Massacre didn't die easily in Azariah Wright, who engaged in a vendetta against Thomas Chandler Jr., son of Judge Chandler. The younger Chandler held political beliefs absolutely in line with Azariah Wright's. Nonetheless, Wright "took against him." In 1779, Chandler was elected speaker of the Vermont House; Wright worked strenuously to get him removed. His letters to the governor and council reveal Wright's tone of mind (and notions about spelling):

> *To his Excellency Governor in Chief, Left Governor and prudent Council of Freemen with Greeting, I send, not forgeting the Independent State of Vermont. Fortitude Good Manners Honisty resolution makes a Free people, not being thoughtless of the fountain from whence &c. Now Gentlemen I beg assistance as one Mr. Pompee of Chester has Borrowed of me the value of Six or Eight Silver Dollars in horse tackling which when required to return the Chief Speaker his Agent Thomas Chandler Esqr answers for him in wrighting. Not Gentlemen that I should grieve myself for the loss of 6 or 8 Dollars, but with and, &c., that said Esqr Chandler should be Chief Speaker for the black Ethiopian not for Whites. if your Honours Can do any thing I should remain your most obedient*
>
> *Azariah Wright.*
> *"put Law in force sift the House."*

As far as can be understood, Wright objected to Chandler's acting as attorney for a black man. His next note makes even less sense:

> *Great is amarica, there terror starts all Yourope, Exolted be Varmount tho Little May be head, and ware the Crown of gustus, ferfull am I of that, while Deceit is att head, Not to condemn the whole, nor gustify any only by marit, it is amazing that People that have ben led to the Slaughter by*

Deceit Should trust the same man for there Councellor, thomas Chandler Esqr I ment, who wrote to Incurrige the ferse Soons of Liberty to assembel att Westminster, Declaring he new his farthers mind, and by Deceit we lost two brave herooes these are to Remind Deceit and Shun Destruction To the Exclet Governors and Councle from your most obedent   Azariah Wright. Westminster March the—14—1780.[127]

What deceit does Wright refer to? On March 13, when the Chester men set off for Westminster, Chandler expressed verbal support for stopping the court of which his own father was a judge, saying that "the attorneys vexed the People with a multiplicity of suits" and the "sheriff of the County was undeserving to hold his office" and "had bad men for his deputies." He was always known for zealously holding this position, and there is no evidence that this was in any way feigned or false. But Wright's fumings were made public and were enough to lose Chandler his speakership in mid-1780.

Chandler sued for £10,000, alleging libel. Wright pleaded not guilty, the jury felt otherwise and Chandler was awarded—not £10,000, but £3. This was increased on review to £6 damages and £216 for cost of the suit.

WESTMINSTER, CAPITAL OF VERMONT

The legislature met in various towns around Vermont two or three times a year for short sessions lasting a few days. Westminster was the meeting place in March 1780; Stephen Rowe Bradley and Nathaniel Robinson represented the town. (Meanwhile, another Westminster citizen, Elkanah Day, was representing Cumberland County in the New York Assembly.)

The 1780 assembly meeting took action on an issue that had troubled the state for over a year. There was no printer within Vermont borders; acts and laws were sent out of state to be printed. The legislature had tried to get Alden Spooner, a printer at Dartmouth College, to "move his press to Westminster without loss of time." But Spooner preferred to remain near the college, and at the assembly meeting at Westminster in March 1780 it was "voted to request the Governor and Council 'to obtain a printer within this State.'"[128]

Stephen Rowe Bradley was appointed to a committee to work on getting a printer. Bradley apparently reached back to his old Connecticut connections and drew up a draft agreement with Timothy Green, the state printer of Connecticut, for presentation at the August 18, 1780 legislative session at Bennington. Green agreed to furnish his son-in-law and former apprentice, Judah Paddock Spooner, and his son, Timothy Green, with type and equipment to set up a printing office at Westminster. He also agreed to back them financially, provided that the two, as partners, "be made official printers to the State of Vermont, and assured of full state patronage, as well as of the financial help that had been offered to Alden Spooner."[129] Alden and Judah Spooner were brothers with a printing office in Dresden, New Hampshire, which for a time during the Eastern Union was considered part of Vermont. They had been named "Printers for the General Assembly of this State" (Vermont) in 1778. Their work was highly competent, which was why the state made such strong efforts to keep Alden as the state printer.

Bradley's draft agreement was accepted. Ezra Stiles, a son of Dr. Ezra Stiles of Yale then living in Westminster, was sent to New London to help move the types and other equipment.

The historic wooden press itself had been brought from England by Stephen Daye in 1638 and set up in Cambridge, where its first job was a broadside of the "Freeman's Oath." It later produced the first American almanac with calculations for New England and an Indian Bible. The press was owned by Harvard College between 1656 and 1714, when it was bought by Timothy Green, who set it up in Connecticut. Later, Alden Spooner moved it to Dresden, New Hampshire (now Hanover). From there it was moved to Westminster by Spooner and Green.

The move went smoothly, and in autumn of 1780, Vermont's

The Stephen Daye Press was brought from England in 1638. It was owned by Harvard, used by Alden Spooner at Dartmouth College and came to Westminster in 1780. *Vermont Historical Society.*

first printing press, and the official state press, was up and running on Westminster's Lower Street. The press office was located in a small building that, according to local tradition, now forms the ell of the Congregational parsonage building on Route 5.

The earliest known work printed by Spooner and Green was the pamphlet *Acts and Laws, passed by the General Assembly of the representatives of the Freemen of the State of Vermont, at their session at Bennington, October, 1780*. The pamphlet was brought out toward the end of November.

Next came the first issue of Vermont's first newspaper, the *Vermont Gazette*, or *Green Mountain Postboy*. The heading of the paper read, "Pliant as Reeds, where Streams of Freedom Glide; Firm as the Hills to Stem Oppression's Tide; Printed by Judah Paddock Spooner and Timothy Green." A contemporary historian dates the first issue as coming out on December 14,

The *Green Mountain Postboy*, printed in Westminster, was Vermont's first newspaper. *Vermont Historical Society.*

1780; later historians have given a date of February 12, 1781. The paper came out weekly for two years and suspended publication in 1783. Only one copy of the newspaper is known to exist. It and the press are in the Vermont Historical Society museum.

First Paper Money

In April 1781 the printing of paper money was authorized, and counterfeiting Vermont-issue bills was made a capital crime. Counterfeiting of paper currency was a serious problem in New England at this time. The job of printing the money was given to Spooner and Green, under the inspection of Mathew Lyon, Edward Harris and Ezra Stiles, and the bills were to be delivered to "Honorable John Fassett, Ebenezer Walbridge, and Thomas Porter, Esquires, a committtee for signing and numbering said bills."[130]

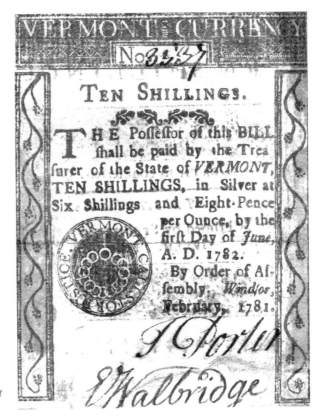

Vermont's first paper currency was printed in Westminster by Spooner and Green. Of the first printing, several bills were stolen and the signatures counterfeited—another Westminster first! *Vermont Historical Society.*

FIRST COUNTERFEITER

On June 13, 1781, Porter and Walbridge appeared before the governor and council to accuse Spooner, Green, Stiles and Samuel Avery, all from Westminster, of counterfeiting. Daniel Martin of Putney had received a bill bearing forged signatures. Martin, perhaps not coincidentally, was a speculator in paper money and was suspected of being connected with a counterfeiting ring.

Spooner and Green were arrested on June 15 at the printing office. Stiles and Avery were arrested elsewhere. Avery and Stiles were questioned and released, but the road was watched for fear they might flee. Spooner and John Gould Jr., another Westminster resident, were questioned on the eighteenth. Gould, then twenty years old, was probably working at the print shop, which he would take over in 1784.

A committee of the General Assembly and the governor and council made further enquiry, employing Paul Spooner and John Fassett to assist. While they were investigating, "a man named Chafee and a boy employed in the printing office, confessed to the crime. The boy purloined the bills and Chafee forged the numbers and signatures."[131] In all likelihood, this was a member of the Atherton Chaffee family, but there is no record of the first name or the name of the boy.

Counterfeiting charges aside, making a living as a printer was apparently difficult in 1780s Westminster. At the end of February 1782, the legislature elected a committee of three men "to Super Intend the press and supply the same." The committee's instructions, dated March 1, 1782, were to "examine the Cause why the printing office has not answered the purposes Expected, and to Engage some Suitable person or persons in the vicinity of Westminster to Supply every Material for the said press on as reasonable conditions as can be obtained, and to engage some suitable post rider or riders to Circulate & distribute the public acts and newspapers through the several Towns in the State."[132] If this couldn't be done, the assembly wanted to move the press to Bennington.

By February 1783, Green had left the business. Another printing office was established in Bennington in mid-1783. Both offices had a difficult time financially, and in 1784, Judah P. Spooner moved his business to Windsor. At about the same time, a judgment is recorded against Spooner, listing him in possession of a house and garden near the courthouse, fifty-four rods of ground on the east side of the street. The sheriff was commanded to "take the body of Judah Spooner and him commit to the keeper of the goal in Westminster and him safely keep until he pays."[133]

John Gould Jr. continued a printing office in the old location of Spooner and Green for many years and printed the first published writings of the youthful William Czar Bradley.

ROYALTON RAID

While Westminster was occupied with printing presses, northern Vermont suffered occasional British raids from Canada. In October 1780, a group of two hundred Indians commanded by a British lieutenant attacked the Royalton area, killing and scalping several people, capturing twenty-five others, burning about forty houses and barns and plundering the countryside. Military units in the Connecticut Valley were alerted by fast messenger, and a battalion of Westminster men under Major Elkanah Day started toward Royalton on October 17. After two days and 30 miles, it became apparent that the raiding party was already far away. A few militiamen traveled on to make sure; among the men serving eight days and traveling 100 to 110 miles were some of Westminster's most martial: Experience and Sylvanus Fisk, Azariah Wright and John Averill. Four men served six days and went 90 miles, among them committed soldier Charles Rice.

LAST CUMBERLAND COUNTY CONVENTION

A convention of town committees from the former Cumberland County was held on October 31. Elkanah Day was named to a committee to look into the feasibility of a new government encompassing the western New Hampshire towns that wanted to be part of Vermont. (Note: This is Cumberland County, Vermont, not Cumberland County, New York; Day seems to have switched allegiance at this point, having given New York dogged service against the odds for many years.)

This effort, known as the Second Eastern Union, reflects complex power struggles between eastern Vermont and the Allens and between rich coastal New Hampshire towns and poor backcountry towns. The Second Eastern Union was controversial and brief. However, Westminster's town fathers seem to have supported it. In Liber C of the Westminster land record books is the following note: "Voted and resolved that this town do highly approve of the proposed union of the whole of New Hampshire with the State of Vermont and accordingly instruct their representatives in General Assembly to endeavor to bring about the same."

THE BROOKLINE FALSE ALARM

Royalton rattled nerves in the Connecticut Valley. On October 31, as the county convention met in Westminster, some hunters on West Hill in Putney spotted surveyors working on the margins of Grassy Brook in Brookline. One hunter jokingly gave several Indian war whoops, and the surveyors fled, telling everyone they met that Indians were coming. Two men cutting wood in Athens also heard the yells and "with true benevolence spread the alarm in all directions."

Athens evacuated in a panic. "Teams were left harnessed in the fields, ovens which were being heated were allowed to grow cool at liesure, and victuals which were being cooked were permitted to take their chances at the blazing hearthstones." Some people in Newfane had taken advantage of the pleasant day to burn brush and old logs. The fugitives spotted their fires at night and imagined that Newfane had been destroyed.

A heavy snowstorm had blown up. Nonetheless, word spread, reaching Westminster by evening. In the morning, the militia under Elkanah Day started for the place where the alarm had started. These were the same men who had marched toward Royalton just two weeks earlier. Other militias marched from other towns.

The snow was deep, the trees bent down in every direction. After wading or snowshoeing for three miles, the Westminster militia decided the Indians must be having an equally hard time traveling. They turned around and marched home again.

Meanwhile, two to three hundred panicked people poured through Putney and went as far as Westmoreland, across the river in New Hampshire. When it eventually became clear that this was a false alarm, they had to return home on almost impassable roads. Most unusually, no militia pay requests were entered for this episode, likely reflecting local embarrassment.[134]

DOMESTIC ASSAULT

In 1780, Miriam Wright filed a domestic assault complaint against her husband, Azariah, alleging that on the evening of December 6 he did "violently assault and beat her"; on December 11 he put her "in fear of her life and safety," "taking his sword and other weapons dangerous" and brandishing them over her.

Azariah Wright was brought before the justices, declared guilty of "a high breach of the peace" and "recognized in the sum of 500 pounds lawful money," to appear before the county court in its next session. There is no record of further court proceedings; Miriam may have dropped charges.[135]

WINDHAM COUNTY CREATED

In February 1781, the Vermont legislature divided Cumberland County in thirds. Windham County was created, essentially with the same boundaries as today. Westminster became the county seat of a much smaller county. A few days later, on February 19, the legislature divided Windham County into half-shires. Courts were to be held alternately in Marlborough and Westminster. Westminster began to lose some of its intrinsic importance as the capital city of Vermont's most populous county. But half the court sessions were still held in Westminster, the county's supply of gunpowder was still stored there, the Vermont press was still there and the jail was still there.

ALARM AT NEWBURY

Only a month later, on March 16, 1781, there was another alarm at Newbury, Vermont, of unknown cause.[136] General Bayley ordered the militia of adjacent towns—and apparently some far-flung towns as well—to march to the place. Two companies of Westminster militia, captained by Jesse Burk and Michael Gilson and under Burk's command, marched fifteen miles toward Newbury. At that point the alarm must have been called off, and they returned home, having been in the service three days.

These alarms account for a high percentage of Westminster's Revolutionary soldiers. Many more citizens of Westminster responded to these dangers—real or imagined—than to the call to fight the British. For most in Westminster, though threats and alarms continued, the war ended with the Saratoga Campaign. In 1781, there was only one Westminster man, Uriah Carpenter, serving in the regular army.

Chapter 7
The Guilford Insurrection

CIVIL UNREST

Westminster was now shire town of both Windham County, Vermont, and Cumberland County, New York, and had a double complement of court officers, including Elkanah Day, sheriff of Windham County, and Timothy Phelps of Marlboro, high sheriff of Cumberland County. Michael Gilson, stubbornly loyal to New York, was appointed a justice of the peace for Cumberland County.

In 1781, a number of former Tories announced their allegiance to America and Vermont and stood for election, among them Benjamin Burt of Westminster. He was elected judge of the county court on March 27. The election of Burt and other former Tories was protested by men in Rockingham and Dummerston, but the legislature chose to uphold their elections.

The political situation was still confused. Semisecret negotiations between Ira Allen and the British were ongoing, and rumors flew. Were the leaders of Vermont in league with the British? Did that make it more patriotic to advocate reunion with New York? It must have been very confusing, and the arguments, especially when influenced by rum punch, must have become extremely tangled.

VOTES FOR NEW YORK

Guilford and Brattleboro in particular turned against the idea of Vermont, creating great turmoil in the county. In March 1782, Brattleboro voted to withdraw from Vermont and return to New York; similar votes followed in

Guilford and Halifax, and committees of the three towns asserted that if other towns, including Westminster, had been allowed to vote, the result would have been the same—a conclusion that is open to doubt. Much correspondence followed between these towns and New York, to the consternation of the Vermont government.

In the summer, Guilford, now the most populous town in Windham County, resisted the Vermont draft. Vermont tried to confiscate property; cows were seized and rescued. Civil government by the state of Vermont had failed.

Meanwhile, New York preserved the fiction of governing its former territory, appointing justices of the peace for the by now defunct Cumberland County. One of them was Michael Gilson of Westminster. They were theoretically empowered to protect the interests and property of New York Loyalists. The former Cumberland County southern regiment was also revived, or at least officers were appointed. The Vermont General Assembly sent a representative to reason with the rebellious towns; when this failed, the legislature prepared for military action.

Allen's Militia

In early September 1782, Governor Chittenden authorized Ethan Allen to raise a force of 250 men to act as a *posse comitatus* in Windham County to restore civil authority. Allen's men arrested Timothy Phelps near his Marlboro home. The Allen forces were augmented by companies of Windham county militia, including men under Colonel Stephen R. Bradley and Adjutant Elkanah Day of Westminster. Day, once a committed Yorker, was now firmly on the side of Vermont.

Allen gathered prisoners at Halifax and marched through Guilford, where his men were fired on. Allen threatened to give no quarter, to desolate Guilford like Sodom and Gomorrah if opposed, and the Guilford men retreated. Allen continued gathering prisoners and sent them under strong guard to Westminster.

Westminster's West Parish militia did not march to join Allen. Ephraim Ranney Jr., their captain, was loyal to Vermont but unwilling to fight his neighbors. (Ranney's father sympathized with New York.) But on the morning of September 10, the militia members decided they should join Allen after all. Ranney refused to lead them, and they marched toward Brattleboro without him. They met the group with the prisoners in Dummerston and joined them in marching to Westminster, where the twenty were put in jail.[137]

The prisoners were tried over the next two days, with Stephen R. Bradley appearing as state's attorney and William Gould as clerk of the court. The arrests had been irregular, so the county took great care to observe all subsequent legal forms. The prisoners were tried for sedition, and the principal leaders were sentenced to over a year in jail, their goods and estates to be seized and sold. Their imprisonment began at Westminster; later, some were moved to Bennington, where they were treated poorly.

The court then extended to itself the power to seize and sell the estates of the Yorkers they hadn't managed to arrest. Colonel Stephen Bradley was ordered to raise one hundred men "by draft or volunteers," half of a two-hundred-man force augmenting Allen's posse. Captain Benjamin Whitney raised a company of eighteen Westminster men to go to Guilford under Colonel Bradley. Just three years prior, Whitney and Elkanah Day had been tried at Westminster for disobeying Vermont laws. Now they were actively enforcing them. It would be interesting to know what brought about the change, but unfortunately we have no papers from either man.

Vermont solders returned to Brattleboro, driving off 150 head of cattle and unnumbered sheep and hogs from the farms of Yorkers.

Elkanah Day was sheriff of Windham County, Vermont, in February 1783, when at a court session in Marlboro, Timothy Phelps, banished from Vermont on pain of death, stepped boldly into the courthouse and asserted his authority as sheriff of Cumberland County, New York. Judge Robinson ordered Phelps arrested. Day was apparently quite taken aback but ultimately, with the support of the crowd, was able to perform his duty.

Mrs. Brush Returns

Peace with Great Britain was declared in April 1783. Soon thereafter, Crean Brush's widow and his stepdaughter, the widowed Fanny Buchanon, returned to Westminster. By now Margaret had remarried, to Patrick Wall, the Tory tailor who may have sewn the clothes she wore into prison to rescue her husband. Wall didn't accompany Margaret to Westminster but went straight from New York City to Shelburne, Nova Scotia, to seek recompense for his losses as a Loyalist. Margaret and Fanny stayed in Westminster.

Elkanah Day owned their former house. Margaret and Fanny may have lived briefly with their friend John Norton at the Tory Tavern; later in the year, they were staying with Stephen R. Bradley, also a friend despite their political differences. Bradley was now married, to Merab Atwater of

Wallingford, Connecticut, and the couple had an infant son, William Czar Bradley. Stephen Bradley had a fascination with Peter the Great and wanted to name the boy Peter, but Merab disliked the name, and William received his unusual middle name by way of compromise.

Margaret Wall hired John Norton to visit her late husband's executor, Goldsbrow Banyar, in New York to sort out the property issues. Many people had purchased or settled on the former Brush lands, and the legal situation was tangled.

Legendary Wedding

Fanny Buchanon, Crean Brush's stepdaughter, was a young widow of twenty-three or twenty-four when she returned to Westminster. She is described as "dashing," of "imperious bearing" and also as "a fascinating woman, endowed with an ease of manner which she had acquired from intercourse with polite society, and possessed of a refined taste and many accomplishments."[138] An upper-class city woman in a small frontier town, she stood out and was probably rather lonely. She and her mother relied heavily on the friendship of Stephen Bradley, the only person in the neighborhood even remotely from their own class.

Ethan Allen frequently visited Westminster, perhaps with printing business, perhaps to visit his Wright cousins. He was also widowed, and he and Fanny were attracted to each other. It was a Hepburn-Tracy romance; the old soldier and the young Tory widow were both strong characters, and sparks flew. John Norton once said to Mrs. Buchanon, "Fanny, if you marry General Allen, you will be the queen of a new state!"

"Yes," she said, "if I should marry the devil, I would be the queen of hell!" (Hall hastens to assure us that Fanny was "on most occasions, soft and gentle in her ways and speech.")

In February 1783, court was in session. Bradley and the judges were at breakfast when Ethan Allen's sleigh pulled up at the front gate. Allen was invited to breakfast. He answered that he had breakfasted at Norton's and stepped into Mrs. Wall's apartments to see the ladies. Fanny, in a morning gown, was standing on a chair rearranging a china closet. There was a little chat and laughter about a cracked decanter—Fanny remaining on her perch—and then Allen abruptly said, "If we are to be married, now is the time, for I am on my way to Arlington."

"Very well," said Fanny, "but give me time to put on my Joseph." This was a fashionable, many-colored coat of the period.

Was Allen's proposal a surprise to Fanny? Had the pair made arrangements earlier? It was certainly a surprise to Bradley's guests when the couple walked in. The judges and Bradley were "smoking their long pipes," according to Hall. Allen walked up to chief judge Moses Robinson, an old friend, and said, "Judge Robinson, this young woman and myself have concluded to marry each other, and to have you perform the ceremony."

"When?" the judge asked.

"Now!" replied Allen. "For myself I have no great opinion of such formality, and from what I can discover, she thinks as little of it as I do. But as a decent respect for the opinions of mankind seems to require it, you will proceed." (He seems to be saying here that they'd rather just live together and were only getting married to satisfy public opinion.)

"General," said the judge, "this is an important matter, and have you given it a serious consideration?"

"Certainly," replied Allen, "but," glancing at Mrs. Buchanon, "I do not think it requires much consideration."

The ceremony then proceeded, until the judge inquired of Ethan whether he promised to live with Frances "agreeable to the law of God."

"Stop! Stop!" cried Allen at this point. Then pausing and looking out of the window, the pantheist proclaimed, "The law of God as written in the great book of Nature? Yes! Go on!" The scene he looked on is today a marshy cow pasture full of cattails and purple loosestrife; what Allen saw in "the great book of Nature" was probably a busy eighteenth-century farmyard, Bradley being a raiser of beef cattle as well as a lawyer.

The wedding was concluded, Fanny Allen's trunk and guitar case were loaded into the sleigh and the newlyweds drove off to Arlington.[139]

Hall may have gotten this story from William Czar Bradley, an infant at the time. Bradley became a friend of Fanny's when she returned to Westminster years later and would have heard this story from her, from his father and likely from several of the other witnesses, who became his colleagues. That gives the details some likelihood of being correct, though doubtless they received a gentle polish from the storyteller's hand.

Guilford Rebellion

The American Revolution was over, but the revolt against New York rule continued. Yorkers were banished by the legislature, and their property was seized. Congress ordered these decisions revoked, a decree that was very poorly received in Vermont. An ugly mood prevailed in Windham County in 1783. At a gathering of Walpole and Westminster men, including Stephen R. Bradley, anger reached such a level that many of the men damned Congress and drank a toast to its confusion and to the health of King George. Bradley asked if his Walpole friends would support Vermont if the Continental army were sent in to enforce the congressional decrees; he declared that Vermont would resist any force sent against it and that the people of Berkshire County, Massachusetts, would assist them.

By midsummer, Guilford was practically an independent republic. Men went openly armed; Guilford residents corresponded with the Vermont and New York governments, and the two parties spied on one another. Hall says, "Social order was at an end. The farm and the workshop were neglected. But for the mutual suspicion that lurked in every eye and burned for utterance on every tongue, one would have supposed that an Indian force was expected…that had vowed to ravage the fields, burn the village, and murder the people."[140]

During this period, soldiers were frequently called on "to go on an expedition to assist the sheriff in Windham County." Several Westminster men served in these expeditions, under Captain Benjamin Whitney. As autumn wore on, both sides engaged in home invasions, kidnapping and theft. The Vermont government could no longer tolerate the situation. A letter from Stephen R. Bradley to the inhabitants of Guilford, promising protection if they would return peaceably to their families, was ignored. To the government of Vermont, it was clearly time for military action.

"How the Pig Ate the Butter"

A detachment of Vermont troops had been under arms since late October to quell outbreaks; they made nighttime arrests and invaded the homes of Yorkers, confiscating the owners' weapons. The officers, including Lieutenant Experience Fisk of Westminster, were quartered at the inn of Josiah Arms in Brattleboro. Fisk was there when the officers were attacked by a mob in November. The ensign of the detachment, Oliver Waters, was kidnapped, clapped in irons and sent to Poughkeepsie. He was rescued by the time he reached Northampton. The rescue party, under the command of Joseph Tucker, took a detour to kidnap Timothy Phelps; they, in turn, were captured and tried in Hadley. The situation was completely out of control, and the Vermont forces gathered for action.

The troops rendezvoused at Josiah Arms's inn starting Saturday, January 17; there were fifty-three from Townshend, forty-four from Westminster, thirty-two from Wilmington, twenty-seven from Putney, twenty-two from Rockingham, twenty-two from Dummerston and fifteen from Marlborough. The Westminster men were under the command of Captain Benjamin Whitney. As the troop passed through Westminster, someone asked Sergeant Sylvanus Fisk, "a young man, rash and impetuous," what he planned to do in Guilford. Fisk said he'd show the Yorkers "how the pig ate the butter."[141]

By Sunday, Brattleboro was a military encampment, with men marching, fifes and drums playing and bullets being molded. Yorkers barred their doors; Vermonters opened them and welcomed the soldiers. By Monday morning, over three hundred men were assembled. Westminster was in the first brigade of militia, under Colonel Stephen R. Bradley.

They started off in a severe snowstorm, in conditions reminiscent of the Brookline scare. The men marched single file, and watchers, seeing man after man pass through distant clearings, got the impression that there were one thousand of them. Guilford had posted guards who carried this exaggerated report back to town.

The soldiers overnighted in houses and barns on the edge of Guilford and, on Tuesday morning, continued south. The first group of forty Yorkers fled at their approach, convinced they faced a mighty army. The next group, ensconced in the house of a widow Holton, was pushed out by Captain Whitney's Westminster men with no shots fired. The men spent the night there and on Wednesday marched on, some to Marlboro and Halifax and the main body following the Yorkers into Guilford. The snow was deep by now; Colonel Bradley and Dr. Elkanah Day borrowed horses so they could better supervise the march.

At the hilltop house of one Packard or Packer (present-day Packer's Corner, site of a famous 1960s commune) about a mile and a half from the Massachusetts line, the Vermonters and Yorkers finally met. The Yorkers, at dinner inside, rushed out with their guns when the Vermonters arrived.

The Vermonters advanced. Squire Packard appeared at his door and begged Sergeant Sylvanus Fisk, temporarily in command, not to come any farther. Once he passed the blacksmith's shop just in front of him, Packard warned, he would be fired on. Fisk ignored the warning and pushed on, triggering two volleys of shots that caused no injury.

As the smoke of the second volley cleared, a man in a blue coat stepped out of the maple trees, took deliberate aim at Sergeant Fisk and fired. The ball entered the right side of Fisk's stomach and passed into his groin. Sixteen-year-old Theophilus Crawford asked, "Are you badly hurt, Sergeant?"

Fisk said, "God bless you! Don't ask any questions, but push on and kill some of these devils." The Westminster men did push on, chasing the Yorkers half a mile across the Massachusetts border.

Meanwhile, Fisk, unable to walk, was carried by sleigh back to Mrs. Holton's house, where presumably he was treated by Dr. Day. At first he was considered likely to recover and was probably brought home to Westminster to his wife's care.

SECOND REVOLUTION COMPLETED

The skirmish at Packard's effectively ended active, armed resistance to Vermont government in Guilford. About twenty prisoners were transported to the Westminster jail. Several leaders of the Guilford insurrection were punished there by whipping and pillory.

> During the sessions of the court Westminster had presented more the appearance of a military encampment than of a peaceful village. With the departure of the dignitaries of the bench, the lawyers at the bar, and the prisoners at the dock, it again assumed its wonted aspect, and the roll of the drum and shrill notes of the fife gave place to the music of the sleigh bells of winter, and left to their jingling notes the monopoly of noise for the rest of the season.[142]

Other Yorkers remained as refugees in Massachusetts, kept from their homes by the presence of troops in Guilford. Forty-plus Westminster men were among those stationed in Guilford until the first of March. According to Hall, the militiamen were apt to consider the property of Yorkers who had fled as "legitimate spoil," and many of the deserted houses and barns in Guilford were looted. Ultimately, through a mixture of harsh measures—banishment, confiscation of property—and leniency whenever Yorkers were willing to mend their ways, Vermont consolidated its hold over the rebellious south. But before it did, a young Massachusetts man, Daniel

Spicer, escorting a Guilfordite home to visit his family, was gunned down and robbed by Vermont militia. This was in March; in June, Sylvanus Fisk, thirty-one, died of his wounds.

Guilford was the last military action of the Revolutionary period for Westminster troops. Though the militia members are listed as Revolutionary War soldiers, this can't be properly be considered Revolutionary War service. That revolution was already over. The fight at Packard's was part of what was essentially a civil war.

This period, like the Westminster Massacre, is apt to be lightly regarded by historians. On the surface, the Cow Wars are amusing, as is the idea of the Republic of Guilford. But at the time these were serious events. Important men, pillars of the church and of their towns, were jailed in Westminster under horrific conditions. New York sympathizers in Guilford were chased from their homes in the dead of winter and were kept away by occupying troops from nearby towns. Their homes were looted by their neighbors. Two young men were killed over the difference in state jurisdiction.

As important as any of the physical and economic consequences were the implications for the idea of political liberty. The colonies had freed themselves from Great Britain. Vermont had freed itself from New York. But freedom only went so far and then ran into the concept of unity. For passionate people who had spent so much of their lives achieving freedom, this was infuriating, blatantly hypocritical and for many must have been a crushing disillusionment. Only the distance of time can make these events amusing and create the impression that Vermont's transition from New York rule was peaceful.

AFTERMATH

Azariah Wright is best remembered for not being excommunicated from the Westminster Congregational Church. According to the widely published story, the church attempted to excommunicate him for shooting a bear in his cornfield on the Sabbath. On the day of the vote, Wright brought his musket into the meetinghouse and, as the excommunication was about to be read, raised it and aimed at Reverend Joseph Bullen. Bullen passed the paper to John Sessions, who declined to read it; Wright is said to have remained a member in good standing until his death.

In fact, Wright was a declared Episcopalian by 1800.[143] While he may have shot a bear on the Sabbath—it would have been like him—he was

The gravestone of Azariah Wright. *Michael Fawcett.*

probably almost excommunicated for his habit of slapping Reverend Bullen whenever they met. Wright sold his farm to Lot Hall in 1785 and moved to a farm in the hills, where he died in 1811. He is remembered in Westminster as Uncle 'Riah, a local hero.

Medad Wright is remembered as a Tory, though there is no evidence for this. He was certainly a loyal Yorker. Grandchildren of Medad and Azariah married each other; their descendants were taught that they were descendants of Azariah Wright; Medad was rarely mentioned.

Thomas Chandler fell on hard times and was imprisoned for debt in the Westminster Courthouse in 1785. There he died a pauper, perhaps in the same cell where French died. At that time, people believed that by touching the body of a debtor you could inherit his debts and also that by carrying the body past the bounds of the jail yard you would be regarded as accomplices in an escape. Chandler's body was left to rot in the June heat for several days. Finally, Nathan Fisk, the jailer, measured the jail "liberties"—the outdoor area where prisoners were allowed to walk—and found that by stretching the surveying chain, he could make the jail yard overlap the cemetery grounds. A grave was dug that began in the cemetery and ended in the jail yard. A few hardy souls slipped into the cell at midnight, put the "putrescent mass"[144] into a rough box and slid it to its final resting place. The grave, like Daniel Houghton's, was never marked, and its whereabouts are unknown.

Vermont was accepted into the Union in 1791, thanks in large part to the efforts of Stephen Rowe Bradley. Bradley became one of Vermont's first two U.S. senators and proposed a flag with fifteen stripes and fifteen stars, honoring Vermont and Kentucky. Known as "the Bradley flag," it flew over Fort McHenry during the War of 1812 and inspired Francis Scott Key to write "The Star-Spangled Banner."

Bradley married for his third wife Melinda Willard, daughter of Billy Willard, one of his clients during his first court appearance in Westminster. Both Billy and his father, William Willard, claimed to be the killers of William French. William Willard apparently died insane of some hemorrhagic disorder; Hall says many Vermonters felt it was poetic justice for the death of French.[145]

The Bradley family crypt, built by Stephen Rowe Bradley in the Old Cemetery in Westminster, overlapped the grave of William French. We have no record of public opinion on this. The French gravestone was later broken and stored in the Old Meeting House, where it was destroyed in a fire in 1888. A replica of the stone now leans against the northeast corner of the Bradley edifice, sharing a place of honor with the stone of Penny, William Czar Bradley's beloved dog.

Fanny Montusan-Buchanon-Allen had several children with Ethan Allen. Following his death, she married Dr. Jabez Penniman and moved back to Westminster; the couple lived

William Willard was believed to be the man who killed French. His granddaughter became Stephen R. Bradley's third wife; his great-grandson owned Willard's Hotel in Washington, where Lincoln stayed before his inauguration. *Michael Fawcett.*

The State of Vermont erected a monument to William French (and Daniel Houghton) in 1873. *Michael Fawcett.*

on Rocky Hill, on the present Connecticut Valley Orchard land. Penniman cared for Stephen R. Bradley's second wife during her final illness. In gratitude, then senator Bradley obtained for Penniman the post of Vermont collector of customs, which he held during the run-up to the War of 1812. He was collector of customs during the infamous *Blacksnake* affair.

Margaret Brush Wall lived to a ripe old age and died in Westminster. Crean Brush's daughter from his first marriage came to Westminster and tried to gain title to the lands Brush had left her; her efforts were largely unsuccessful.

In 1787, Newfane was made the county seat. The Westminster Courthouse was used for various purposes, including in 1794 a school where Daniel Hall, father of the historian Benjamin Hall, studied. It was demolished about 1806, by order of the town, by Tory John Norton and Revolutionary silversmith Isaiah Eaton. Some of the timbers were reused in Westminster houses; the bullet-riddled door gathered cobwebs in the Stoddard family barn for over a century, until Westminster regained an interest in its history and took measures to preserve it.

The Vermont legislature voted to erect a monument to William French and Daniel Houghton in 1872. The monument was inaugurated in 1873.

William French is considered Westminster's martyr, though he was a Brattleboro boy. It was a Westminster boy who boasted of killing him, but Westminster rarely mentions that. Danel Houghton is nearly forgotten, and Sylvanus Fisk is completely so.

Appendix
Later Views of the Massacre

A Sampler

Minutes of a Dummerston meeting of August 22, 1775, contain the following view of events at what the "Records of Dummerston" called "that blood Stained Star-chamber in Westminster." Houghton was a Dummerston man, French nearly was and Dummerston was a hotbed of anti–New York feeling.

> *Votid that it tis the SenCe of this toun that the Letters that are in the hand of Dr. Soloman Har-vy are Not any EvidanCe in the Case which the Commite is Colecting for the Evidance whiCh tha are to ColeCt is the the Bad ConduCt of the Cort from its fust Setting up the Cort Doun to the fust of MarCh Last and that those Letters only Shye that the Peple ware Displeaised at the Earbitrary ConduCt of offiseirs of the Cort and ware Reday to Rise and Stop the Cort be fore that time: and those Lettors Show Like wise the unity of the People and purfix the time: and we think it Best not to have those Letors go to Westminster.*

From a Dummerston meeting on February 26, 1776:

> *Votid to Send a man to Jine the County Comittee on the twelfth of marCh at the hows of Mr. John Sergants at Brattleborough at Nine of the o Clock in the fore Noon to Draw up a Remnonstrance to Send to the Contanalshall Congress at Phile Dalpha Consarning those that perpatratid the Bloody Massacree on the thirteeinth of march Last.*[146]

From an Ira Allen pamphlet in 1777:

> *In open violation to the laws of the crown, the legislative and executive powers, assumed to themselves authority to hold courts: their conduct was so notorious that it was the cause of that odious and never to be forgotten massacre at the Court House in said Cumberland, on the evening of the thirteenth of March 1775, in which several persons were actually murdered. O! horrid scene!*[147]

A Stephen Rowe Bradley pamphlet of 1780, titled *Vermont's Appeal to the Candid and Impartial World*, made the case for Vermont statehood:

> *But above all they* [the people of Vermont] *suffered, from the cruelty of Great Britain and her emissaries.—For the truth of these things we can appeal to many undeniable facts. So late as March, 1775, previous to the battle of Lexington, the judges of New York, were led in fetters of iron, within the gates of their own city, for shedding innocent blood at Westminster, in murderously attempting to enforce the laws of that province upon the people of Vermont.*[148]

Six years after the Massacre, in protesting the election to office in Windham County of some Tories and Yorkers, some Rockingham residents declared that these men had been "active and accessory in shedding the first Blood that was shed in America to support Brittanic Government, at the Horrid and Never to be forGot Massacre Committed at Westminster Cortt House on the Night of the 13th of March, 1775. O horred Cean." Strongly derivative of the Ira Allen pamphlet, it also may be the earliest "first blod" claim regarding the Massacre. Many Rockingham men were in the courthouse that night.[149]

From a view from 1781 (Hall does not give an author) opposing Vermont's annexation of thirty-five New Hampshire towns:

> *That unhappy event so occasioned the addition of Spirit and numbers to the opposers of that Government as enabled them to effect their design. The People concerned in that transaction, Supposed themselves to be engaged in the Common cause of the Colonies, and generally expected the Court party to be opposed to the same, and as many of them proved afterwards either from principle or by reason of what they esteemed persecution, proved to be Tories, this served to give a more plausible colouring to the truth of the above*

supposition. In addition to the Name of Tories which the generality of the Court supporters had obtained, the Title of Yorkers was joined, and to serve a turn were made synonymous. The other part of the People under the direction of some warm Leaders always inimical to New York, taking advantage of the times when this and York state who each had claims of Jurisdiction over them, were busily engaged against the common Enemy, did erect themselves into an Independent State by the name of Vermont. The Yorkers were pretty generally deniers of the pretended authority of said Vermont State and acted as they were able under the Government of New York.[150]

In 1852, the report of the Select Committee of the Vermont House of Representatives chosen to advise the House on appropriating money to build a memorial to French had the following to say:

It remains only to add, that with the burial of William French, were buried the hopes of subjugating the men who dwelt on the hills and in the valleys of the Green Mountains. The spirit of resisting oppression to the last extremity, awakened by his death, was never extinguished, and within two years from that time, there was proclaimed from the same building in which he was martyred, the Declaration of the Independence of Vermont.

How far the conflict in that house, on the 13th of March 1775, led to the heroic determination of the Patriots of Massachusetts, which in about one month from that time displayed itself in the skirmishes at Concord and Lexington and afterwards in the battle fires of Bunker Hill, can never be known, but your committee fully and firmly believe that they have the undeniable warrant of History that the blood of William French was the first which flowed for American Independence in our Revolutionary struggle.[151]

Committee members were George W. Grandey, George Lyman, Jarvis F. Burrows, Hiram Ford and Thomas Browning.

Benjamin Hall's views:

The events of 13th of March have been styled in these pages a mob, a riot, and an affray, names chosen by the crown adherents to express their idea of the nature of the transactions of that day. The term "massacre" was the more dignified title employed by the Whigs to convey their own notions of the same proceedings. A more correct conception is conveyed by the word insurrection. The people rose against civil and political authority, and in so doing were justified on principles which do not admit of dispute...

First, there was oppression on the part of the government against which resistance was finally made; secondly, every peaceable means, by petitions and remonstrances, for removing this oppression, had been tried, but in vain; thirdly, forcible measures were not resorted to until the probability of success had become so strong as to amount, for the time being, almost to a certainty. Trusting thus to the justice of their cause, and to the favor of Him who is ever ready to succor the oppressed, these determined men resolved to achieve for themselves the blessings of independence, and laid the foundations of those institutions which are the characteristics of a republican government.

In claiming for William French the title of the proto-martyr to the cause of American liberty and of the Revolution, it may chance that but few will be found willing to allow him such an honor. Lexington and Concord point with pride to their battlegrounds, and Charlestown boasts of her Bunker Hill, on whose top towers the symbol of our national strength, the genius of America. But amid these noble memories it should never be forgotten, that on the plains of Westminster the cause of freedom received its first victim, and that in his grave were buried all hopes of reconciliation with the mother country.

When the Grecian warrior consulted the oracle at Delphi, wishing to know whether the Athenians or Spartans would conquer in battle, the priestess gave answer that the army would be victorious in which a soldier was first slain; for she well knew that his comrades would not tire in the struggle until the death of the first martyr had been avenged by the defeat of his and his country's foes. And thus, when on the side of Liberty and the American Colonies the proto-martyr fell, every wound in his body became a mouth which called for vengeance, and from every drop of blood there sprang forth a hero, not in embryo, but armed, to battle bravely for his country.[152]

It's not generally known that Hall was a grandson of Westminster. His grandfather, Lot Hall, moved to Westminster in 1782 and bought Azariah Wright's homestead. Benjamin's father grew up in Westminster, and his connections allowed the historian to talk with family members of participants in the Massacre.

The site of the courthouse was marked with a stone monument in 1902. Judge H.H. Wheeler gave the historical address:

As an object of peculiar interest and appropriateness, he [Judge H.H. Wheeler] showed the audience the original court docket of Cumberland

Now on a private driveway, the courthouse marker is rarely seen. It was moved when Courthouse Hill was paved and only approximates the location of the courthouse. *Michael Fawcett.*

County, containing the record of the New York courts held at Chester and afterwards at Westminster. The court proceedings stopped short with the Westminster incident, and when the courts were resumed under the independent State of Vermont the book was turned over and entries resumed at the other end.

Judge Wheeler especially impressed on his hearers the fact that this attack was not the work of a mere mob, influenced by antipathy to New York and draughts of New England rum, but that it was the serious and determined expression of the growing opposition to the harsh exactions of English rule. "Within a month, at Lexington, was 'fired the shot heard round the world'; here at Westminster was fired a shot heard at least part way around the world." Before the Westminster incident there had been fracases in Boston, in Rhode Island, and elsewhere. Here at Westminster was shed the first blood of the Revolution.

Alfred S. Hall, Esq., also addressed the crowd. A Boston lawyer descended from the West Parish Halls, he framed the Massacre within a discussion of the land dispute with New York, yet he notes:

**Officers of the Brattleboro Chapter
Daughters of the American Revolution**

••

Regent, MRS. EDWIN H. PUTNAM.

Vice Regent, MRS. ANNIE G. COBB.

Recording Secretary, MRS. WILFRED F. ROOT.

Corresponding Secretary, MISS GENEVIEVE SLATE.

Treasurer, MRS. CLARENCE F. R. JENNE.

Registrar, MRS. EDWARD A. STARKEY.

Historian, MISS MARIA STEDMAN.

Chaplain, MRS. FRANK W. WEEKS.

Auditors, MRS. HENRY P. WELLMAN,

MISS MARY E. SMITH.

Committee on Marking

MRS. C. F. R. JENNE,

MRS. F. W. WEEKS,

MRS. H. D. HOLTON,

MISS STEDMAN,

MRS. E. H. PUTNAM.

Field Meeting
of the
**Brattleboro Chapter
Daughters of the American Revolution
and Citizens**

Court House, March 3, 1775

**Westminster, Vt., on site of the Old Court House
Wednesday, September 17, 1902**

HENRY D. HOLTON, M. D., PRESIDENT OF THE DAY

Order of Exercises

••

Basket Collation, 12 o'clock

••

MUSIC. THE BAND.

PRAYER. REV. G. D. DeBEVOISE.

ADDRESS OF WELCOME. GEO. C. WRIGHT.

RESPONSE. HENRY D. HOLTON, M. D.

HISTORICAL ADDRESS. ALFRED S. HALL, ESQ., Boston, Mass.

SINGING. THE CHILDREN.

UNVEILING OF MARKER. HOLLIS AND HELEN WRIGHT.

EARLY HISTORY OF SOUTHERN VERMONT.
JUDGE H. H. WHEELER.

SHORT ADDRESSES. HON. K. HASKINS, and others.

SINGING, AMERICA.

Committee of Arrangements
at Westminster

••

STEPHEN M. NUTTING,

BRIGHAM T. PHELPS,

JOSEPH H. UNDERWOOD,

GEORGE N. BANKS,

FRED I. LANE,

MRS. STEPHEN M. NUTTING,

MRS. OCTAVIUS L. FISHER,

MRS. GEORGE H. WALKER.

Marshal, BRIGHAM R. PHELPS.

Aids, SETH ARNOLD AND WALTER C. NUTTING.

Selectmen of Westminster

LUCIUS C. RICHARDSON, JOHN B. MINARD, JOSEPH P. RANNEY.

The DAR program for the courthouse marker dedication ceremony in 1902. *Westminster Historical Society.*

But Westminster, Putney, Chester, and some other towns near the Connecticut river, had been re-chartered by New York about 1772, and the land trials between New York and the settlers, though not forgotten or without an influence on the minds of the men, at this time could not have been the potent force which determined the common people to oppose the holding of a court at Westminster on March 14, 1775.

"There were deeper reasons and fresher grievances."

He cites the resolutions passed by the Continental Congress and adopted by Cumberland County, as well as the maladministration of the courts. After describing the Massacre, he says:

> *Thus on the thirteenth day of March, 1775, the fatal shot had been fired by British authority, vested in the officers of the court of colonial New York, upon peaceful, but organized and determined, resistants of that authority. Five years before this, men had been slain in Boston by British soldiers, who indiscriminately fired upon a mob; and a monument is erected to their memory on Boston common. Here there was no mob, but an organized insurrection; and here was shed the first blood of an organized body of men resisting Great Britain in the Revolutionary War.*[153]

In 1927, the Honorable Frank L. Fish gave an address at the Vermont State Sesquicentennial Celebration at Westminster on January 15:

> *What did the people arm themselves with clubs for? Because they thought they might have to resort to force to hold the court-house. Force against whom? The King; and the King came in the night in the person of his sheriff, and a posse of men armed with clubs and guns, and they drove out the people's party, whose clubs were no match for powder and lead, and took possession of the King's court-house. They killed my kinsman William French, mortally wounded Daniel Houghton, injured several others, and imprisoned quite a party in the King's jail. Court met next morning in the King's court-house and adjourned until afternoon. It adjourned then, never to meet again. The King had departed forever from Westminster.*
>
> *The order of his going was not of his choosing either. Armed men liberated his prisoners. They seized and imprisoned his guardians of the law. They took them a little later, to make more certain of holding them, a hundred miles under a guard of soldiers and locked them in a stronger prison than that at Westminster, over which they had no jurisdiction whatever. And here at Northampton...they left the King in jail. Events must be judged by what follows as well as what precedes them.*
>
> *When the armed party left Westminster, taking with them by force all that represented kingly authority that had had to do with the massacre, what was going on here? The streets were filled with soldiers. They had gathered in popular uprising on hearing of the massacre, in defense of the interests of the people—from Massachusetts Bay, from New Hampshire and from Vermont. There were half a thousand of them. Those who first met the*

shock of arms in the battles of Concord and Lexington were but a handful compared to them in numbers. The massacre was the result of a protest against the arrogance of the King, and it resulted in events so revolutionary that when viewed in the light of what preceded and followed it is impossible to dissociate it with the Revolution itself.

…What had preceded that fateful day? All the acts of British oppression of which the colonists complained. The challenges from the eloquent lips of American patriots. The meeting of the Continental Congress and its declaration of rights. Assemblies everywhere up and down the colonies to protest against the mother country. Already Masachusetts was in rebellion and the King's troops were in readiness to strike the first blow. The revolution was lodged everywhere in the hearts of liberty-loving men and it needed but the right touch to make the issue one of force. That first touch came in Westminster where the first organized opposition to the King's authority was exercised. That opposition was an armed opposition, organized by the people to ward off the King's officers should they attempt to possess the King's court house. The King's men made an attack on the home guard and blood was shed. We must decide whether those who shed

Courthouse Hill. The courthouse stood at the top, near the center of the road. Houghton died in the Harlow house, to the right of the road. Stephen R. Bradley's farm was at the bottom of the hill, on the right. *Michael Fawcett.*

their blood here were a "mob" as the King's party were pleased to call them, or whether they were a part of that great movement for human liberty which resulted in our independence. I prefer the latter interpretation, and I like to attach Westminster to Concord, and Lexington, and Bunker Hill, and Hubbardton, and Bennington, and Saratoga, and all the other fields made red by American blood shed in the cause of liberty; and I like to think of the young man whose sister's blood flowed in my mother's veins as the first martyr to that cause.[154]

Sherman, Sessions and Potash, in their 2004 Vermont history, *Freedom and Unity*, state:

For the first time, moderate easterners listened intently as Cochran declared the "Westminster Massacre" an uprising against New York tyranny and offered the services of the Green Mountain Boys to assist their new eastside allies in avenging the blood spilled…The Westminster affair signaled the end of New York's continued operation of courts or any other institution in the Grants. Henceforth, as advocates for violence gained the upper hand throughout the colonies in their determination to throw off the continued injustices of British rule, their calls to remember the "Massacre" significantly bolstered the cause of independence.[155]

The Massacre has been reenacted by children from the Center School several times since 1981. However, it has lost a good deal of its luster and status. The word "massacre" is often spoken with a chuckle; we require more than two corpses for a massacre these days. But in 1970, no one caviled at calling the shootings at Kent State and Jackson State massacres. The similarities are strong: armed agents of the government firing point blank into a crowd of unarmed protesters. The emotions roused by those events may help us understand why Westminster has always been called a massacre, sans quotation marks.

Though the event was called a "massacree" from the beginning, it might help modern people understand it better if we began to call it "the Westminster Insurrection." Arguably, Westminster was the first place where the entire apparatus of His Majesty's colonial government was overthrown. For more than two hundred years, the town has considered itself an important Revolutionary War site. The Westminster Massacre in 1775 was followed by Vermont's Declaration of Independence in 1776. It's no wonder some Westminsterites take exception to Windsor's self-designation as "the birthplace of Vermont."

One of the most striking things a close study of the era reveals is how like today it was. People switched sides—or their positions "evolved." It was complicated. After a few pints of cider, it was probably impossible to decipher local politics without a diagram. People had mixed motives. They recast their stories to show their side in the best light; a ragged drunken volley became careful warning shots. Each side threw the other into prison under appallingly crowded conditions. Each side employed "artful lawyers."

And then, amazingly, people got over it. The Tory John Norton became a respected town official, just like the Whig Nathaniel Robinson. Westminster healed, tore down the courthouse and moved on.

But we remember.

Notes

DEDICATION

1. Benjamin H. Hall, *History of Eastern Vermont from Its Earliest Settlement to the Close of the Eighteenth Century* (New York: D. Appleton & Co., 1858), 752; from an anonymous ballad published in 1779.

CHAPTER 1

2. Hall, *History of Eastern Vermont*, 58.
3. *Bellows Falls Times*, undated clippings.
4. William A. Haviland and Marjorie W. Power, *The Original Vermonters; Native Inhabitants Past and Present, Revised and Expanded Edition* (Hanover, NH: University Press of New England, 1994).
5. Esther Munroe Swift, *Vermont Place Names: Footprints of History* (Camden, ME: Picton Press: 1977), 498.
6. Hall, *History of Eastern Vermont*, 81–82.
7. Westminster Historical Society Collection.
8. *Souvenir Edition of the* Bellows Falls Times, *Devoted to the Towns of Walpole and Westminster, Historical, Industrial, Biographical* (Bellows Falls, VT: W.C. Belknap & Co., July 1, 1899).
9. Walter Hill Crockett, *Vermont, the Green Mountain State*, 5 vols. (New York: Century History Company, 1921–23), 281.

10. Michael Sherman, Gene Sessions and P. Jeffrey Potash, *Freedom and Unity, A History of Vermont* (Barre: Vermont Historical Society, 2004), 81.

11. Crockett, *Vermont*, 296–97.

12. Vermont 1771 Census.

13. Hall, *History of Eastern Vermont*, 752–53.

14. "Petition of Certain Parties to be Reannexed to New Hampshire," reprinted in *Controversy between New York and New Hampshire Respecting the Territory Now the State of Vermont, Documentary History of the State of New York*, vol. 4, compiled by E.B. O'Callaghan (Albany, NY: C. Van Benthuysen, public printer, 1849–52), 412.

15. Simon Stevens, Samuel Wells, Oliver Willard and John Kelly, reprinted in *Controversy between New York and New Hampshire*, 423–29, 430–31.

16. Chilton Williamson, *Vermont in Quandary 1765–1785* (Montpelier: Vermont Historical Society, 1949), 19.

CHAPTER 2

17. *Vermont History* (Summer/Fall 2002): 70.

18. David Burton Bryan, PhD, "Mother and Daughter: The Lives of Fanny Montresor and Fanny Allen" (unpublished manuscript, 1990).

19. Pronunciation note: Fanny was pronounced "Fanna" in old-time Vermont, according to David Bryan, citing evidence from the Allen Family Papers no. 959: Ira sends greetings to "Miss Fanna" (Bryan, "Mother and Daughter," 203). This sheds light on the large number of men named Bela in early Westminster, such as Bela (Billy) Willard, and on William Czar Bradley's youthful nickname, "Billa Czar."

20. Bryan, "Mother and Daughter," 218.

21. Hall, *History of Eastern Vermont*, 605.

22. Ibid., 175.

23. Rev. F.J. Fairbanks, *The Double History of Westminster, Vermont: The History of the East Parish, Vermont Historical Gazetteer, Windham County*, vol. 5, edited by Abby Maria Hemenway (Chicago, 1867), 9.

24. Hall, *History of Eastern Vermont*, 184.

25. R.S. Safford, "Remarks on Vermont's Centennial Celebration," *Argus and Patriot*, January 31, 1877.

26. Hall, *History of Eastern Vermont*, 185.

27. Ibid., 719.

28. Ibid.

29. Ibid., 604.

30. Sherman, Sessions and Potash, *Freedom and Unity*, 90.

31. Hall, *History of Eastern Vermont*, 605–6.

32. Ray Raphael, *A People's History of the American Revolution; How Common People Shaped the Fight for Independence* (New York: Harper, 2001).

33. E.P. Walton, *Records of the Council of Safety and Governor and Council of the State of Vermont, to which are prefixed the records of the General Conventions from July 1775 to December 1777*, vol. 1 (Montpelier, VT: Steam Press of J. & J.M. Poland, 1873), 315.

34. Hall, *History of Eastern Vermont*, 199.

35. Ibid., 198.

36. Ibid., 204–5.

37. Reuben Jones, *A Relation of the Proceedings of the People of the County of Cumberland and Province of New York*, Slade's *Vt. State Papers*, 55–59, American Archives, Fourth Series, 1775, vol. 2, cols. 218–22. Journals of the General Assembly of the Province of New York.

38. Hall, *History of Eastern Vermont*, 202.

39. Ibid., 202, quoting Slade's *Vt. State Papers*, 56.

40. Hall, *History of Eastern Vermont*, 203–3, from Dummerston records, 18–20.

41. Hall, *History of Eastern Vermont*, 206.

42. Jones, *Relation of the Proceedings*.

43. Ibid.

44. Ibid.

CHAPTER 3

45. Ibid.

46. Ibid.

47. Hall, *History of Eastern Vermont*, 233.

48. Ibid., 235.

49. Jones, *Relation of the Proceedings*.

50. Ibid.

51. Ibid.

52. Ibid.

53. Ibid.

54. Hall, *History of Eastern Vermont*, 228–29, 231.

CHAPTER 4

55. Jones, *Relation of the Proceedings*.

56. Ibid.

57. Thomas Chandler et al, "State of the Facts," in Hall, *History of Eastern Vermont*, 746–47.

58. Hall, *History of Eastern Vermont*, 233.

59. John Griffin, deposition sworn before Judge Daniel Horsmanden, April 5, 1775, reprinted in *Controversy between New York and New Hampshire*, 548–50.

60. Oliver Church and Joseph Hancock, depositions sworn before Judge Daniel Horsmanden, March 22, 1775, reprinted in *Controversy between New York and New Hampshire*, 544–48.

61. Hall, *History of Eastern Vermont*, 224.

62. Ibid., 229.

63. Church and Hancock, deposition.

64. Ibid.

65. Ibid.

66. Ibid.

67. Ibid.

68. Hall, *History of Eastern Vermont*, 227.

69. Ibid., 753.

70. History Committee for the Halifax Historical Society, *Born in Controversy; History of Halifax, Vermont* (Halifax, VT: Itty-Bitty Publishing, 2007), 197.

71. Hall, *History of Eastern Vermont*, 231.

72. Griffin, deposition.

73. Hall, *History of Eastern Vermont*, 233.

74. Ibid., 237.

75. Ibid., 238.

76. Ibid., 239.

77. Ibid., 720.

78. Ibid., 729.

79. Ibid., 246.

80. Samuel Wells, William Paterson and Samuel Gale, "Petition of the Civil Officers of Cumberland Co.," reprinted in *Controversy between New York and New Hampshire*, 552–53.

81. Eleazer Patterson, Samuel Knight, Benjamin Butterfield, John Sergeant and Josiah Arms, "Petition of Col. Patterson and his Fellow Sufferers," reprinted in *Controversy between New York and New Hampshire*, 614–15.

82. Hall, *History of Eastern Vermont*, 234–35.

83. Manuscript, Westminster Historical Society.

CHAPTER 5

84. Ken Stevens, "Abijah Moore's Company of Cumberland County Militia," in *New England Historical and Genealogical Register* 150 (July 1996).

85. Alfred Stevens, *The Double History of Westminster, Vermont: The History of the West Parish; Vermont Historical Gazetteer, Windham County*, vol. 5,edited by Abby Maria Hemenway (Chicago, 1867), 78–79.

86. Walton, *Records of the Council of Safety*, 340.

87. Hall, *History of Eastern Vermont*, 244.

88. *American Archive, Fourth Series*, vol. 3, Columns 429–31.

89. Hall, *History of Eastern Vermont*, 251–52.

90. *Souvenir Edition of the* Bellows Falls Times. Quoting Henry C. Lane, great-grandson of Azariah Wright.

91. Bertha Miller Collins and Frank Miller, *Vignettes of Westminster, Vermont*, edited and compiled by Rachel Valliere Duffalo (Westminster, VT: Westminster Historical Society, 1994), 69.

92. Bryan, "Mother and Daughter," 49.

93. Ibid., 209, citing O.P. Allen.

94. Hall, *History of Eastern Vermont*, 623.

95. Ibid., 609–24.

96. Ibid., 246–47.

97. Sherman, Sessions and Potash, *Freedom and Unity*, 99.

98. Jonas Fay, clerk, *Reports of Governor and Council: Report of Adjourned Session at Dorset, Sept. 25, 1776*, 35.

99. Walton, *Records of the Council of Safety*, 48–50.

100. Ibid., 47.

101. Ibid., 51.

102. Mrs. Jenkins, *United Opinion* (Bradford, VT, March 28, 1941); source was a descendant of Bildad Andross.

103. Photocopy in Westminster Historical Society collection, original owned by Ed Sawyer.

104. John E. Goodrich, *State of Vermont Rolls of Soldiers in the Revolutionary War, 1775 to 1783* (Rutland, VT: Tuttle Company, 1904), 35, #300.

105. Ibid., 40, #206.

106. Ibid., 665.

107. David Perrin, *Coin Silver: Is It a Vermont Mark?* (Charlotte, VT: self-published, 2005), 5–6; information from Vermont Historical Society file 61.63.

108. Hall, *History of Eastern Vermont*, 624–25.

109. Walton, *Records of the Council of Safety*, 366.

110. John Sessions, reprinted in *Controversy between New York and New Hampshire*, 572.

111. Hall, *History of Eastern Vermont*, 310–11.

112. Ibid., 325.

113. Ibid., 756.

114. Ibid., 627.

115. Mary Greene Nye, comp., *State Papers of Vermont, Volume Five, Petitions for Grants of Land 1778–1811* (Brattleboro: Vermont Printing Company, Inc., by authority of Rawson C. Myrick, Secretary of State, 1939), 109.

116. Hall, *History of Eastern Vermont*, 628.

CHAPTER 6

117. Ibid., 334.

118. Ibid., 336–37.

119. Ibid., 344.

120. Ibid., 339.

121. Mary R. Cabot, *Annals of Brattleboro, 1681–1895* (Brattleboro, VT: E.L. Hildreth & Co., 1922), 109; Hall, *History of Eastern Vermont*, 340.

122. Hall, *History of Eastern Vermont*, 340.

123. Ibid., 342.

124. Henry Kellogg Willard, *Willard-Bradley Memoirs* (n.p.: privately printed, 1925), 30.

125. Ibid., 34.

126. Ibid., 36.

127. Hall, *History of Eastern Vermont*, 731 (both letters).

128. John Spargo, *Reprints from Vermont History: A Collection of Articles of Lasting Interest About Vermont's Early Days* (Montpelier: Vermont Historical Society, 1975), 110.

129. Ibid., 111.

130. Ibid., 112.

131. Ibid., 113.

132. Ibid., 113–14.

133. Westminster land records, Liber A.

134. Hall, *History of Eastern Vermont*, 396–98.

135. Ibid., 732.

136. Ibid., 408.

CHAPTER 7

137. Ibid., 445.
138. Fairbanks, *Double History of Westminster*, 27–28.
139. Hall, *History of Eastern Vermont*, 629–31.
140. Ibid., 500–1.
141. Ibid., 518.
142. Lyman Hayes, *Connecticut River Valley*, quoting a Westminster resident, 88.
143. Westminster land records, Liber H.
144. Hall, *History of Eastern Vermont*, 584.
145. Ibid., 753.

APPENDIX

146. Ibid., 750.
147. Ibid.
148. Ibid.
149. Ibid.
150. Ibid., 751.
151. Ibid., 240.
152. Ibid., 240–41.
153. Alfred S. Hall, "Address on the Marking of the Site of the Old Court House," September 17, 1902, 5.
154. Hon. Frank Fish, "Address on the Vermont State Sesquicentennial at Westminster," January 15, 1927.
155. Sherman, Sessions and Potash, *Freedom and Unity*, 94.

Index

About the Author

J essie Haas grew up in Westminster on the farm owned in Revolutionary War times by John Wells (a member of Azariah Wright's militia and a soldier in the Continental army). She lives adjacent to that farm with her husband, Michael J. Daley, in an off-grid cabin they built themselves. A graduate of Wellesley College, Haas is the author of over thirty award-winning books for children and young adults, including several historical novels.

Visit us at
www.historypress.net